THE ROTHSCHILD RHODODENDRONS
A RECORD OF THE GARDENS AT EXBURY

The Exbury FCC form of *Rhododendron lutescens*

THE ROTHSCHILD RHODODENDRONS

A RECORD OF THE GARDENS AT EXBURY

C.E. Lucas Phillips and Peter N. Barber

Drawings by Gillian Kenny
Photographs by Harry Smith
With a foreword by The LORD ABERCONWAY v.m.h.
REVISED EDITION

MACMILLAN PUBLISHING CO., INC.
NEW YORK

Macmillan Publishing Co., Inc.
866 Third Avenue, New York, N. Y. 10022

Library of Congress Catalog Card Number: 79–88036
ISBN 0–02–597440–8

First American Edition 1979

PHOTOTYPESET BY BAS PRINTERS LIMITED,
WALLOP, HAMPSHIRE, ENGLAND
PRINTED IN HOLLAND BY
VAN LEER & CO LIMITED

To Mrs Lionel de Rothschild

*(though she passed away in 1975, we leave
the dedication unaltered in this edition)*

Contents

PART FOUR RHODODENDRON CULTURE

List of Illustrations

PHOTOGRAPHS (Those in colour are by Harry Smith)
Frontispiece   The Exbury FCC form of *Rhododendron lutescens*

The Drawings

The flower drawings by Gillian Kenny are from specimens grown at Exbury.

FOREWORD by The Lord Aberconway
Victoria Medal of Honour

In the years between the two world wars Lionel de Rothschild and my father competed keenly with each other in showing their rhododendrons and other plants. At the same time they were the best of friends, sharing a love of gardens and of plants, and encouraging each other in the pursuit of their common hobby.

Lionel, as he would like still to be thought of, started gardening after 1918, and during the next twenty years achieved and maintained a unique position in horticulture. He created at Exbury a magnificent garden, in which he planted rhododendron hybrids he had raised, rhododendron species introduced from expeditions he had generously supported, and shrubs and trees of almost every genus suitable to the climate of Exbury. His gardening was in the grand manner; he raised upwards of 500 rhododendron cultivars, most of them improvements upon their parents, and indeed, in deciding his breeding programme, showed uncanny skill in assessing which qualities in a parent would be dominant, and which recessive, and therefore what would be the likely outcome of a particular cross. He not only made beautiful his corner of the world, but by his generous gifts of plants enriched many gardens in Britain and overseas, and brought much pleasure to many visitors to shows.

When he died in 1942 the more pressing preoccupations of the war prevented his work from receiving its full and proper recognition. The gardeners of the world owe much to him.

It is therefore fitting, and I am delighted, that a record of his gardening achievements has been compiled in the form of this excellent book. It is a work of considerable horticultural importance and much research has gone into it. It will be cherished and consulted wherever rhododendrons are loved or studied. Indeed Mr Smith's superb illustrations alone may open to many a new understanding of the breadth and scope and fascination of the genus rhododendron.

Lionel would have greatly approved of this book. Even more he would have approved of how his work has been carried on with love and understanding by his widow, by his elder son, and by Peter Barber, one of the authors of this book.

Origins & Acknowledgements

FIRST EDITION

The main bases for this record of the work of the late Lionel de Rothschild are his stud-book and his own numerous writings, together with the personal testimonies of Mrs Lionel de Rothschild and their son and his wife, Major and Mrs Edmund de Rothschild, and we are accordingly grateful for having had this information at our disposal. A list of other sources is given at the end of the book.

We wish likewise to thank Mr F. P. Knight, Director of the Royal Horticultural Society's Garden at Wisley, for kindly reading the manuscript of this book and making several valuable suggestions from his own wide knowledge of rhododendrons and of Lionel de Rothschild in person. Mr H. H. Davidian, B.Sc., of the Royal Botanic Garden, Edinburgh, and Mr C. D. Brickell, B.Sc., the RHS botanist, have been good enough to check the botanical detail and to read the proofs. Miss A. V. Brooks, B.Sc., the RHS plant pathologist, and Mr J. Forsyth, B.Sc., lately the entomologist, have similarly checked the detail in the section on the ailments of rhododendrons. Mr James Russell has also kindly read the manuscript and Mr Ambrose Congreve has helped with information.

We are further very much indebted to Mrs Fred Wynniatt for her help in preparing the groundwork for the Register contained in Part III, a laborious work that has greatly lightened our own task.

The Council of the Royal Horticultural Society have kindly authorized us to quote extracts from *The Rhododendron Handbook*, the Rhododendron and Camellia Year Books and other publications of the Society and we record our thanks accordingly.

REVISED EDITION

The original edition of this work, published in 1967, brought the record of Exbury up to May 1966. This revised edition carries it on to the end of 1977. The introductions and awards since 1966 are shown at the end of the main Register and the book has been brought up to date in the treatment of diseases and pests and in various matters of other detail. We have had valuable help from the scientific staff of the RHS, from the Society's publications and from Mr Douglas Harris, now Managing Director of Exbury Gardens.

We should like to point out that Mr Brickell succeeded Mr Knight as Director at Wisley in 1969.

C. E. L. P.   P. N. B.

Rhododendron Terminology

The methods of naming all plants are governed by the ordinances of an international body.[1] A few points, as far as they concern rhododendrons, are set out here for the benefit of those not familiar with them.

A **grex** (Latin for flock, herd, troop, etc., abbreviated to g.; plural, greges) is the international term for a collection of seedlings from the same parentage. Such seedlings, while sharing the general characteristics of the grex, may vary in colour, quality or other particulars. The term is falling into desuetude since the first edition, but is retained here.

A **clone** name (abbreviated to cl.), as applied to rhododendrons, belongs to one seedling only in the grex and its own progeny raised by vegetative means (cuttings, layers and grafts, not by its own seed).

The same name may often appear for both a grex and a clone. Thus 'Hawk' is a grex name for all the seedlings resulting from the cross *R. wardii* × 'Lady Bessborough', first made by Lionel de Rothschild. The first exhibited seedling of this cross was itself named 'Hawk' and this seedling is a clone. Subsequently other seedlings from the same grex were exhibited and were at that time named simply 'Hawk' variety 'Kestrel', 'Hawk' variety 'Merlin', etc. Under the ordinances now reigning, however, 'Kestrel' and 'Merlin' are described as clones of the Hawk grex.

Other variations on the 'Hawk' theme were developed from fresh crossings of the same parents, such as the celebrated 'Crest', but they are still members of the Hawk grex.

Similarly, another raiser bred from *thomsonii* × *griffithianum* and named the progeny 'Cornish Cross', which is a grex name. Rothschild made the same cross himself and the resulting clone is now given cultivar status as 'Exbury Cornish Cross' (formerly 'Cornish Cross Exbury variety').

In *The International Rhododendron Register* many clones are alphabetically separated from the greges to which they belong (e.g. 'Crest' and 'Exbury Naomi'). In the Exbury Register incorporated here, however, this practice has not been followed and all the known clones of a grex are shown together under the grex name, including those not raised by Lionel de Rothschild.

Variety (abbreviated to var.) is a term sometimes considered best reserved for variations originating in the wild in a true species. Thus in *Rhododendron thomsonii* var. *pallidum* the flowers are paler than the red of the species. The term **forma** is sometimes used for a simple colour variant. The names of genus, species and variety are printed in italic.

[1] The International Commission for the Nomenclature of Cultivated Plants of the International Union of Biological Science, Utrecht. Their rules are formulated in the International Code of Nomenclature for Cultivated Plants.

Cultivar (abbreviated to cv.) is an international term for variations of the species, or categories of plants subordinate to the species, that have originated in cultivation, as distinct from those that have originated in the wild. Their names are written between single inverted commas. A clone is one form of cultivar. All rhododendron hybrids dealt with in this book are cultivars.

However, under the International Code, the use of the term "cultivar" is entirely optional and the English term "variety" is explicitly declared to be the "exact equivalent" of it (as also are the equivalents in other languages). Accordingly the more familiar vernacular word will normally be used in this book. It should be noted, none the less, that the Royal Horticultural Society has adopted the formal international style.

Other terms that will be met are:

Indumentum. One of the stratagems devised by rhododendrons in the wild to regulate the release of water vapour from their systems, especially during the spells of dry weather that are so dangerous to them. It consists of a growth, particularly on the underside of the leaf, of fine, soft hairs, which may be as tenuous as cobwebs or as firm as felt. The colour of this indumentum is usually in tones of light or dark brown, or it may be yellowish, grey or sometimes white.

The indumentum is often a means of identification and it may also be an attractive feature of the plant, especially when an indumentum dresses the young shoots overall in spring with a soft plush-like raiment, shaping them into handsome chestnut cockades, as in *R. bureavii*, or into soft white rabbits' ears as in *R. yakusimanum*, or into other decorative styles, as in Lionel de Rothschild's 'Fusilier', 'Fortune', 'Grosclaude' and several more.

Another group of rhododendrons has evolved a system of minute scales, which we may liken to valves opening and shutting at need. Scales of a different nature may be found on the buds and stems also. Some rhododendrons have both scales and a hairy indumentum. The scaly group are known as lepidotes and those without scales as elepidotes. The lepidotes and elepidotes are, with rare exceptions, maritally incompatible.

Another form of protection is a covering of rather waxy papillae. All these methods of moisture control are known as trichomes and are examined in detail by Dr J. MacQueen Cowan in *The Rhododendron Leaf*.

Lobe. One of the sections or "petals" that make up the bell, trumpet, funnel or tube of the whole corolla of a rhododendron flower. Most species and varieties have five lobes, but they may number anything from four to ten.

Nomenclature. A group of botanical theorists, headed by Edinburgh Royal Botanical Gardens, is proposing yet another new method of naming rhododendrons, but we do not agree with it.

Part One Narrative

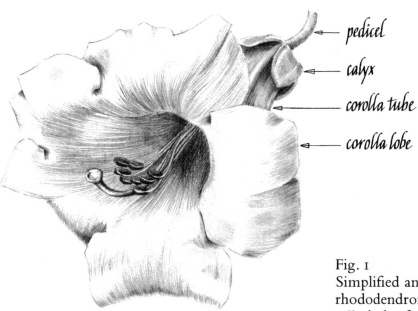

pedicel

calyx

corolla tube

corolla lobe

Fig. I
Simplified anatomy of a
rhododendron floret (*R. lindleyi*,
a "tubular funnel-shaped" style).
The Exbury AM form is flushed
with pale rose-magenta towards
the apices of the lobes.

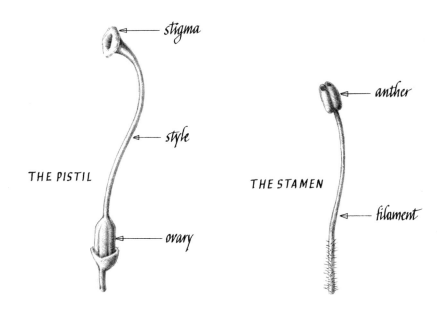

stigma

style

THE PISTIL

ovary

anther

THE STAMEN

filament

Narrative

Until fairly recent times the rhododendron used to be considered by the world at large as a plant suited mainly to large estates. Parks, woodlands and broad acres were thought to be their appropriate *mise-en-scène* and deep pockets their means of procurement. On a smaller scale, but on a level yet more choice and rarefied, the rock gardener, drinking in the heady phrases that raced through the pages of Reginald Farrer, cherished his alluring pygmies on peaty terraces and within the clefts of stony outcrops.

The First Species

The plant discoveries in Asia in the last century and the hybrids resulting from them had opened up a new gardening era, of which Britain was the main pioneer. Its development was slow and confined in the main to the large estates; but "the appetite grew by what it fed on" and a new outburst of plant-hunting expeditions in distant regions of primitive and romantic beauty became financed by men of wealth, by horticultural institutions and by the more eminent nurserymen. The austere heights of the Himalayas, the sumptuous mountain forests of Assam and Upper Burma, the remote hills of the deepest Chinese hinterland, the islands of Japan, the fringes of the Arctic Circle, the tropical forests of Java and Sumatra— these and many other lands where nature had planted the rhododendron countless centuries before the emergence of man were searched at peril of human life for the adornment of the gardens of Britain.

At the time of Charles II only one rhododendron was in cultivation. This was *R. hirsutum*, which had been introduced into England in 1656 from the European Alps and was accordingly known (like *R. ferrugineum*, which did not come until a century later) as the "Alpine Rose". These are perhaps the only two known to grow naturally in limestone soils but are no longer considered choice of their kind.

By 1800 there were still only twelve species known, some of which had been found by the settlers in America. Then, in 1811, there arrived in England a distinguished immigrant from the Himalayas that was to have a profound and prolonged influence on Western gardens. This was the magnificent red form of *R. arboreum*, which was quickly seized upon by the pioneer hybridists and which took so kindly to certain parts of Britain that there is today a specimen in Cornwall towering up to some sixty feet.

It was not until the middle of the century, however, that the great wealth which lay hidden in the mountains of Asia began to be fully revealed, when Sir Joseph Hooker made his great pioneering expedition to the Himalayas and brought to the world a wholly new conception of rhododendrons with such sumptuous species as *R. falconeri*, magnificent in its stature, foliage and pale gold, undercut bells; *R. griffithianum*, its large, white bells dappled with green, tinted pink and beautifully veined; *R. thomsonii* with blood-red flowers, emphatic calyx and rufous bark; *R. cinnabarinum*, highly distinctive in its slender, pendent trumpets; and *R. campylocarpum* with bells of pallid primrose and small, glossy leaves, all in due time to make their contributions to Lionel de Rothschild's most distinguished creations.[1] And from China in 1856 Robert Fortune sent back the

[1] Related and illustrated in the sumptuous *Rhododendrons of Sikkim-Himalaya*, by Joseph Dalton Hooker, edited by his father, Sir William Hooker, 1849.

ambrosial *R. fortunei* to become the father of Lionel de Rothschild's stunning 'Naomi' and of Sir Edmund Loder's now classic 'Loderi' and all its children.

Thus by 1900 some 300 species had come to be known, but there still remained to be explored the richest of all rhododendron hunting grounds in the world—the remote and forbidding mountains of the inner heart of China. The first revelation of their hidden wealth had been made by the French Catholic missionaries, David, Delavay and Farges, who spread their nets in the fields of botany and zoology as well as among the souls of men. But it was Dr Ernest Wilson who, financed by the great London nursery of James Veitch and Sons, made the first systematic exploration at the turn of the century. From then onwards a flood of new discoveries poured in from the successive expeditions of a great company of collectors voyaging among the mountains and shaley valleys of Asia, often among hostile inhabitants, across trackless and precipitous hills, threatened by fierce storms and floods.

George Forrest and Reginald Farrer died on their arduous expeditions, but their work was carried on by Captain F. Kingdon-Ward, Dr J. F. Rock, the partners Ludlow and Sherriff and others. In this golden age of plant hunting China and its borderlands yielded their most sumptuous treasures, to be greeted by the West with amazement and delight and to provide our own and other gardens with new colours, new forms and a season of flowering that extended to half a year.

Here came in the dwarf rhododendron species *williamsianum, leucaspis, russatum, scintillans, keleticum* and *pemakoense*. Here arrived the large and splendid *macabeanum*, growing forty feet high in the primitive beauty of its native Manipur (so soon to be the scene of ferocious fighting between Slim's soldiers and the invading Japanese), the equally tall *sinogrande*, with leaves sometimes a yard long, the twenty-foot *discolor*, so valuable for late blooming, and a host of others that are today the foundations of the great rhododendron estates or of many small rock gardens.

The number of known species has thus swollen to about a thousand; no doubt yet more riches would have been discovered if China, on becoming Communist, had not put down its "Bamboo Curtain" to hide its secrets from the inquiring West.

The First Hybrids

While all these treasures of the wild were being gathered in, preponderantly to Britain in the first place, the hybridizers were also busily working to produce new forms and qualities. Derived as they were from such diverse homelands, many of the species did not at once take kindly to the average conditions of Western Europe and still less kindly to the usually harsher conditions of North America, when in due course that continent began to take an active interest. Acid soils, a plentiful rainfall and an atmosphere more or less humid were their main demands. Many needed the filtered sunlight of woodland terrain and were not sun-hardy. Others were not frost-hardy, a weakness that was particularly displayed in the northern and eastern regions of North America.

It was from North America, however, that a few of the most hardy, if least beautiful, species had been imported into England in the seventeenth century. It was from two of these that Michael Waterer seems to have made the first known deliberate cross when, in 1810, we are told, he mated *R. maximum*, which is hardy even in Canada, with *R. catawbiense*, whose pale magenta blossoms clothe the western mountains of North Carolina in primitive splendour and of which Waterer's aged specimen still clings tenaciously to life in the Knap Hill Nursery that he had founded.[1]

The arrival from the East of *R. arboreum*, however, was the signal for the beginning of a new era. By 1831 J. R. Gowen had produced the first hybrid from it, under the name 'Altaclarense', a Latinized version of Lord Caernarvon's home, Highclere Castle. Four years later a turning point in history was reached when Michael Waterer, having crossed *R. arboreum* with *R. caucasicum*, gave a delighted world the variety 'Nobleanum', which begins to flower before the winter is over and which still adorns many gardens in its red, pink or white forms. A spate of *arboreum* hybrids followed, but many inherited the tenderness of that parent and the *Gardeners' Chronicle* declared in 1855 that "they never bloom till they are twenty years old". Later in the century, the Knap Hill Nursery produced the first really hardy, dark red hybrid in the celebrated 'Doncaster', an ideal rhododendron for small gardens, now as then.

Hardiness had been achieved and in 1853 Waterer exported 1,500 of his hybrids, many of which had American sap in their cells, to the United States, where they made a stunning impact and where, with others of their kind that followed, they still constitute the standard varieties in the eastern States today. The era of the "hardy hybrid" or "ironclad" rhododendron had begun. Though they may not today be considered connoisseurs' varieties, they have the virtue that they will endure low temperatures and many of them will also suffer without blanching the full heat of the sun in temperate zones.

By the time that the First World War had darkened the horizons of the world in 1914 many splendid rhododendron gardens had been fully established. In Britain there were those of Lady Aberconway[2] in Wales, of J. C. Williams at his story-book castle of Caerhays in Cornwall, of his cousin P. D. Williams at Lanarth, of Sir Edmund Loder in Sussex, Sir John Ramsden at Bulstrode Park, J. B. Stevenson at Ascot, Admiral Heneage-Vivian at Clyne Castle (celebrated for its large-leaved hybrids), and the several luxuriant gardens on the west coast of Scotland.

In America Samuel Parsons and others were similarly diligent; in Germany

[1] Mr. Donald Waterer is unable to confirm the 1810 mating.
[2] Owner of Bodnant. The first Lord Aberconway took no interest in horticulture and Lady Aberconway allowed their son, The Hon. Henry McLaren, to run her garden. It was he who became the famous gardener. For the sake of convenience, future references to "Aberconway" are to Henry McLaren, though he did not succeed to the title till 1934.

Otto Schultz (on *griffithianum* hybrids) and in Holland, Koster, Endtz and Van Nes. A "rhododendromania" infected the horticultural mind. Acres of aucubas and laurels that had soberly clothed mid-Victorian gardens were ripped out to make way for the gaily dressed newcomers. "Monkey puzzles" fell to the axe in large numbers. And the rhododendron began to infiltrate adventurously into the smaller gardens.

In Europe the war of 1914–18 put out of most men's minds the inessentials of life, but with its conclusion a new figure appeared quite unexpectedly upon the rhododendron stage and within a very short time was occupying the centre of it.

"L. de R." Lionel Nathan de Rothschild, a cadet of the English branch of the historic international bankers, was born to Leopold and Marie de Rothschild on 25 January 1882 at Ascott, a country mansion at Wing, Leighton Buzzard. His father, besides being a banker, was a man of wide and warm interests, a celebrated sporting figure and winner of the Derby with St Amant in 1904. Lionel was sent to school at Harrow, where Winston Churchill had preceded him by a few years, and then to Trinity College, Cambridge, before joining the family business of N. M. Rothschild and Sons.

The young Rothschild took an early dislike to the hunting and racing which so much coloured life at Ascott and which brought to its ample portals many of the leading sporting personalities of the day. Instead, somewhat to the surprise of the family, he took a very early interest in flowers. Indeed, at the age of about five years he was given his own small garden, an experiment in human education which seldom fructifies but which in this boy's breast stimulated an ardour that grew with the years. Bird life also very much attracted him. Not that the gentler interests of life alone drew his enthusiasms, for later on he took to motor-cars when they were still in their infancy and was numbered among the pioneers of motor-racing both on land and on water. He was also a good shot, but in later life lost his interest in shooting game.

He grew up to be a good-looking young man with lively blue eyes, outwardly reserved but warm-hearted within. As he matured he became decisive and somewhat autocratic in manner, exceptionally tenacious in the pursuit of his purposes. Whatever activity he engaged in, his was the dominant personality. He could be curt and occasionally quick-tempered, but to the world at large he showed great charm and was a very generous friend. He took positive pleasure in sharing with others the good things that lay at his command and was always ready to lend his powerful aid to a deserving project. The atmosphere that he created, at least during his Exbury days, may be inferred from the fact that he was invariably referred to, by everyone with whom he was not on terms of closer intimacy, simply as "Mr Lionel", including his own staff. He still is, so that even today it is difficult to write of him as "Rothschild".

Lionel de Rothschild

He had an exceptionally quick eye and developed very soon the instincts of a connoisseur and, whether in flowers, motor-cars, or anything else, the factor that he always looked for was quality. Though no expert, he knew much of pictures and other works of art. He played a good hand at cards. His table became renowned for what Lord Aberconway called the "consummate skill" of its preparations, for, though personally abstemious, he regarded cookery as an art and studied it as such. He drank only the finest wines and personally gave orders to his chef every morning for the day's bill of fare.

In 1912, when he was thirty, Lionel de Rothschild took a step that led him into the most significant era of his life. He married Marie Louise Beer, who was a descendant of Meyerbeer, and he bought the small estate of Inchmery.

About twenty miles from Southampton, nine from Brockenhurst and some miles even from any village of significance, Inchmery lies at the mouth of the little Beaulieu River, where the skirts of the New Forest trail out to meet the waters of the Solent. Across the Solent the low, green mound of the Isle of Wight forms a near horizon and Cowes itself is just visible from Inchmery.

Between the island and the mainland there flowed a busy maritime commerce of all sorts. Great liners passed on their way from Southampton to the ports of the world. Europe's most splendid yachts wore their burgees and spread their sails for Cowes Regatta, where King George V, the Sailor King, himself took the helm of *Britannia* and assembled round him the leaders of society of half Europe. Craft of every kind trafficked to and fro and, just obscured by the Isle of Wight, in the great dockyard of Portsmouth lay the warships of the world's most powerful navy.

For in 1912 Britain and her Empire were in the heyday of their greatness and their affluence. The pound, minted in gold by the Rothschilds themselves (for the Royal Mint Refinery was, and still is, their property), was worth twenty-five shillings in the foreign market and there was no paper money less than the crisp, white "fiver". The United States were scarcely yet reckoned among the "Great Powers". It was the most civilized era in international history, when rules of seemly behaviour governed the relationships of most peoples. In Britain, an easy elegance, good manners and good humour suffused society and, by and large, a cheerful industriousness mellowed the temper of a nation at peace.

Such was the environment in which Lionel and Mariloo Rothschild began their joint life at Inchmery. In that remote and pastoral setting, when the automobile was still in its infancy, only an occasional motor-car other than their own Rolls-Royce or Napier penetrated the narrow lanes that twisted among the scattered country houses and farms bordering the Beaulieu River and the southern fringes of the New Forest.

The wild ponies wandered at will (as they still do) across the road and about the countryside. A few adders were to be found (as they still are) among the fallen forest leaves. Special ordinances governed (as they still govern) the rights of those who lived on William the Conqueror's chase. The horse, the carriage, the farm cart and the bicycle ruled the untarred lanes, shying away from the rare motor-car.

The population was sparse and concerned mainly with the service of the land, on which the great shire horses drew the plough, the harrow and the whirling harvester. Even as late as 1932 Lionel was describing this corner of the country as "inaccessible" to anyone without a car.

The Rothschilds' immediate neighbour, two miles away at Exbury House, where he enjoyed one of the finest pheasant shoots in Europe, was Henry Forster, a leading member of Parliament and a first-class cricketer. Four miles to the north of Forster, his wife's brother, who was John, second Lord Montagu of Beaulieu, lived at Palace House, adjoining the ruins of the ancient Cistercian abbey of Beaulieu. Montagu shared with L. de R. his enthusiasm for cars and motor-boats and one of the attractions that had brought Lionel to this remote corner of England had been the opportunity for motor-yachting that was offered by the Beaulieu River and the Solent. Sometimes in partnership, sometimes separately, they won several of the more coveted trophies and in 1907 they had jointly won the Perla del Mediterraneo, when they had broken the world water speed record of 28 m.p.h. Later on Lionel acquired a sailing yacht also.

The little river, wandering tortuously between wide-set banks through a flat landscape, had a peculiar, fenny fascination flavoured with the tang of history, for at Buckler's Hard, on its western bank, about opposite Exbury House, had for generations been built the wooden men-of-war of England. Here Henry Adams and his sons built more than fifty ships that sailed and fought in all the seas of the world in the great days of Britain's maritime prowess. Many won renown in Nelson's day and among them were his own *Agamemnon* (which had been Rodney's before him and in which Nelson lost his eye at Calvi), besides *Illustrious*, *Indefatigable*, *Swiftsure* and *Victorious*, all ships of the line of first rating whose names shine brightly in the pages of the Nelsonic age.

During the week Lionel de Rothschild and his wife lived in London, at 46 Park Street until 1927 and then at 18 Kensington Palace Gardens (now part of the Russian Embassy) and Lionel was, of course, occupied with the family banking business at New Court in the City; but week-ends found him and his wife nearly always at their new Hampshire home. He had already been raising rhododendrons, by simple methods of trial and error, before his marriage, for he planted at Inchmery a quantity of seedlings that he had raised in his parents' garden at Gunnersbury.

Less than two years later, however, the war of 1914 burst upon a shocked Europe. L. de R.'s thoughts, like those of everyone else, turned upon the new immediacies. He was a major in the Buckinghamshire Yeomanry, but, to his chagrin, he was not allowed to go overseas, for his professional services in England were deemed more valuable, especially when he became head of the firm in 1917. In 1916 his first son, Edmund, was born in London, but in the following year Lionel lost his father, Leopold. During the war his uncle Alfred de Rothschild also died, leaving him his estate of Halton, but Lionel did not like Buckingham-shire and Halton began a new usefulness as a training establishment of what shortly became known and renowned as the Royal Air Force.

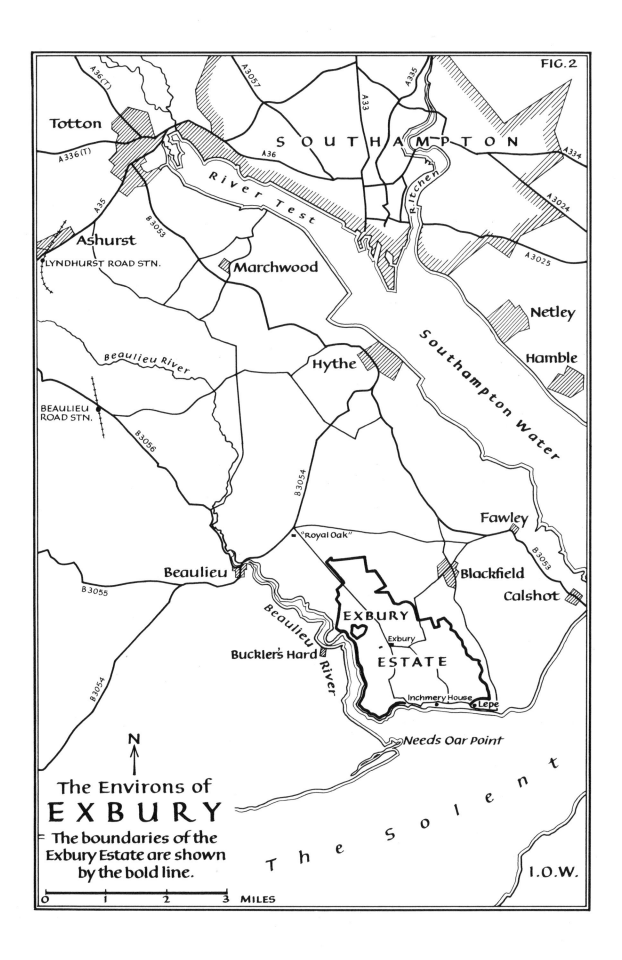

FIG.2

Totton

A36(T)

A3057

A335

A33

A335

SOUTHAMPTON

A36

A336(T)

A35

B 3053

R. Itchen

A334

A3024

River Test

A3025

Ashurst

LYNDHURST ROAD STN.

Marchwood

Netley

Hamble

Beaulieu River

Hythe

Southampton Water

BEAULIEU
ROAD STN.

B 3056

B3054

Fawley

"Royal Oak"

B 3053

Beaulieu

B 3055

Blackfield

Calshot

EXBURY

Exbury

Beaulieu River

ESTATE

Buckler's Hard

B 3054

Inchmery House

Lepe

Needs Oar Point

N

The Solent

The Environs of

EXBURY

The boundaries of the
Exbury Estate are shown
by the bold line.

I.O.W.

0   1   2   3   MILES

Exbury

The war over, Lionel de Rothschild was at last able to bend his large energies to his private ambition. In May 1919 he bought Harry Forster's place hard by at Exbury House, acquiring the whole estate of 2,600 acres, which included several farms and the hamlet of Exbury itself. Forster was very soon afterwards raised to the peerage and appointed Governor-General of Australia.

Exbury House stood on a slight elevation commanding the flat lands of the Beaulieu estuary, with the Isle of Wight in the distance. It was an agreeable but not distinguished small mansion of brick, built by the Mitford family in the early nineteenth century and in need of repair after the war's neglect. As Lionel de Rothschild and his wife stood on the lawn on their first inspection, she looking rather forlorn at its neglected state, he said: "Come, let us explore the grounds. I want to find the two *Cupressus sempervirens* mentioned in Lord Redesdale's memoirs."

Each with a billhook in hand, they hacked their way through a glade dense with scrub and sycamore saplings and found the trees. They bore very old labels saying they had been grown from seed from a wreath that had fallen off the Duke of Wellington's funeral car in 1852, an historical association that delighted Lionel.

Fortunately other fine trees were there also. Close to the house were some majestic cedars of Lebanon of great age and vigour, their strong limbs sweeping out in level tabulations. The tall spires of wellingtonias pointed to the sky. *Magnolia salicifolia* was in its full bridal attire. The April sun gleamed on the copper trunks of Scotch pines. Silver firs stood like ships' masts in a green ocean. Fine old specimen planes and beeches spread wide their heavily clothed limbs. An ancient plane had layered itself and its sturdy progeny, springing up in a circle around it, were shooting outwards at rakish angles, as though anxious to escape from their parent.

Native forest trees abounded also, predominantly the oaks of the New Forest, but all were being jostled by saplings and coarse undergrowth. The soil, though extremely variable, was mainly New Forest gravel, with expanses of clay here and there, but its stony heart was softened by centuries of leaf-mould. Moreover, the soil was acid, with bracken growing abundantly everywhere. Proximity to the sea and river charged the air with some degree of humidity.

Both house and garden therefore offered a promising prospect to their new owners. The house was enlarged, reconstructed and faced with stone, with a shallow colonnade of ten pillars and a crowning pediment and balustraded cornice in the classic manner. What had been an old-fashioned country home became a stylish residence. A specimen *Magnolia grandiflora* growing on the old house was carefully preserved. Beside the front door on the new west face the spreading evergreen *M. delavayi* was planted and grew with such vigour in that mild climate that in time it obscured the lower windows and recently had to be removed.

Three years were occupied in the reconstruction of the house and it was not until May 1922 that the Lionel Rothschilds were able to move in. Meantime,

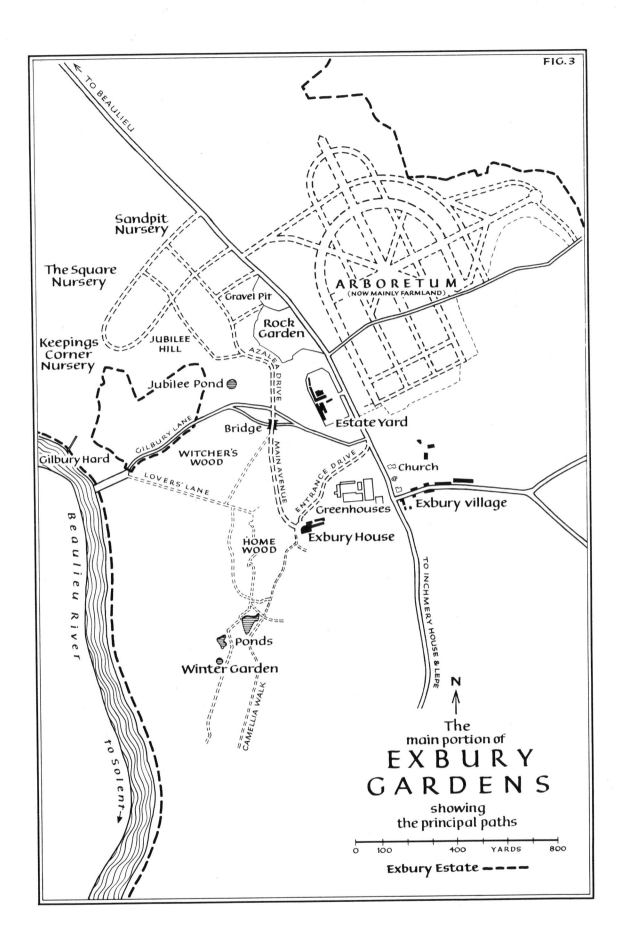

FIG. 3

TO BEAULIEU

Sandpit
Nursery

The Square
Nursery

Gravel Pit

ARBORETUM
(NOW MAINLY FARMLAND)

Rock
Garden

Keepings
Corner
Nursery

JUBILEE
HILL

AZALEA DRIVE

Jubilee Pond

GILBURY LANE

Bridge

Estate Yard

Gilbury Hard

WITCHER'S
WOOD

LOVERS' LANE

MAIN AVENUE

ENTRANCE DRIVE

Church

Greenhouses

Exbury village

Beaulieu River

HOME
WOOD

Exbury House

TO INCHMERY HOUSE & LEPE

Ponds

to Solent

Winter Garden

CAMELLIA WALK

N

The
main portion of
EXBURY
GARDENS
showing
the principal paths

0   100   400   YARDS   800

Exbury Estate — — — —

however, Lionel had begun energetically to transform that part of the estate which most claimed his enthusiasm. In the first year he cleared and planted the ten acres or so of the Home Wood, stretching from the house itself past the three picturesque small ponds nearly down to the oozy bank of the Beaulieu River. From this beginning the garden was rapidly extended until it covered about 250 acres, but was cleft in two by Gilbury Lane.

He proceeded to rip out the crowded saplings, the hazels and the wild under-growth that had provided cover for pheasants, to drive a broad avenue through the core of the woods, to unify the estate by a handsome balustraded stone bridge over Gilbury Lane and to reticulate the woods with twenty-six miles of paths, most of them wide enough for the Armstrong-Siddeley car that he drove at speed, whizzing breathlessly round sharp bends and in-and-out the bushes. The shotgun of the sportsman was silenced and in its place the chink of axe and billhook echoed through the woods.

An enormous transformation took place. A labour task-force of 150 men, coming in from the scattered hamlets for miles around and known as the "trench-ing team" began, on the sites that Lionel ordained, to dig the ground two spits deep, mixing peat with the soil as they returned it, but using no manure or artificial fertilizer. They were apart from the regular staff of sixty trained gardeners employed in the woods and the fifteen in the greenhouses and they went on digging so for ten years.

In addition to the reconstruction of Exbury House, a large building programme was begun with another task force of 200 men under Mr J. M. Johnson, Lionel's clerk of works. The little hamlet of Exbury was doubled in size to provide housing for his regular staff, for Lionel cared for his men; and the unmarried journeymen gardeners were exceptionally well boarded in a bothy that was a model of its kind. Close to the hamlet, long ranges of greenhouses and frames extending to some two acres were built in brick and teak, with stabling for several horses adjoining. The teak, delivered in baulks thirty inches square and twenty to thirty feet long, was processed in Lionel's own sawmill. So was the oak cut from his own trees. A hundred and fifty tons of steel were fashioned by his own blacksmith for the metal fittings of the greenhouses. The four natural ponds were drained, their beds remade in concrete and refilled. In the roof-timbers of all structures, other than the green-houses, only oak was allowed. "Only the best", were Lionel's orders for all materials.

Everything was done on a lavish scale, without counting the cost, but there was no ostentation and everything, except for the floral embellishments which this whole effort was designed to support, was severely practical in style.

Though the natural conditions were otherwise favourable to the creation of a great garden, Exbury lacked the plentiful rainfall of the west coast so propitious to the culture of rhododendrons in particular. It was one of the driest as well as one of the mildest parts of England. "It never seems to rain at Exbury in summer," he complained. There were, however, underground springs draining into the Beaulieu River and fortunately the water was acid. Boreholes were accordingly sunk, providing a quarter of a million gallons daily, which were distributed through twenty-two miles of piping, with sprinklers so placed that no part of the garden should lack water in periods of drought. Of the astonishing creation of the rock garden we shall read later.

Thus piece by piece the woods were thinned, the ground double-dug, the water laid on. In place of the dense undergrowth there were now open glades among the trees. The sunlight filtered through the branches on to the ancient leaf-mould and on to the new shrubs from all quarters of the globe that quickly took root in it. So that when Lionel and his wife moved into Exbury he might well have said, as King Duncan said to Macbeth:

> I have begun to plant thee, and will labour
> To make thee full of growing.

Thus at his first house-warming party he was able to show his guests the first phase of his transformation. On that occasion they included Lord Bessborough (later Governor-General of Canada), Alexander Cadogan (later British representative at the United Nations), Edwin Montagu, Secretary of State for India, the Brazilian Ambassador and their wives. Among rhododendrons he was able to show them a collection of the well-known hardy hybrids with which he began, such as 'Ivery's Scarlet', 'Mme de Bruin', 'Doncaster', 'Ascot Brilliant', 'Gill's Crimson', 'Boddaertianum', 'J. G. Millais', 'Dr Stocker' and so on.

Together with these were many species, which included the glistening white *R. mucronatum* (*Azalea ledifolia*); *arboreum* in its various colour forms; the wan *calophytum*, which was to give him the superb 'Avalanche'; the sweetly-scented *discolor*, which he had already mated with *auriculatum* in 1920, to give him in due course the beautiful 'Argosy'; the freckled, pale pink *sutchuenense* and some good forms of *augustinii* in various tints of nearly true blue, in which he was to take particular interest, as well as, among others that he mentions in his notes, *neriiflorum*, *falconeri*, *fictolacteum* and *eximium*.

Not that Lionel de Rothschild's garden enthusiasm was restricted to rhododendrons. His interests were very wide and it will be convenient for the purposes of our narrative if they are recorded here before coming to the larger subject. He was fond of all trees and shrubs and, in addition to his 250 acres of rhododendrons, planted an arboretum in which he began a collection of every tree likely to be hardy in England and of which his chief counsellor was W. J. Bean, the Curator of Kew Gardens.

In the rhododendron garden itself he planted many more fine trees, including many superb magnolias, among them the great tree-like *M. macrophylla*, and *M. campbellii* (now fifty feet high), dogwoods of all sorts but especially *Cornus florida rubra*, maples of many species, liquidambars, their bronze and crimson foliage challenging the many-tinctured delights of the maples, *Taxodium distichum*, the swamp cypress, its knobbly "knees" jutting up among azaleas, primulas, irises, griselinias and bamboos to encircle the larger of the sylvan ponds; the elegant *Cercidiphyllum japonicum*, with a seat beneath the shade to admire the pond, many conifers large and small, nyssas in quantity, glorious in their autumn plumage, the thorny, fern-leaved gleditschia, the white and gold bounty of the eucryphias, including the new E. × *nymansensis*, the beech-like nothofagus in considerable variety, of which he was very fond, and a host more of handsome strangers sharing the hospitable Hampshire soil with the native oaks and silver birch.

Among the lower-statured shrubs, Lionel was particularly fond of those that enlivened the autumn scene with berries; chief among them he liked cotoneasters, of which he made large plantations. He hybridized here also, and raised two of the finest cultivars now to be found (but found all too rarely). These are the evergreen *C.* 'Rothschildeanus' and *C.* 'Exburiensis', both bearing yellow berries and of graceful and willowy habit. Both came from a crossing of *C. salicifolius* with *C. frigidus* 'Fructu-Luteo'. The splendid, red-berried, fast-growing *C.* 'Cornubia' also originated at Exbury, but not from a deliberate mating. Barberries and pyracanthas added to the berry theme and, at a lower level, the opaline pearls of *Pernettya mucronata* and the dark purple fruits of *Gaultheria shallon* here and there densely clothed the ground.

Added to these was a varied host of other shrubs—viburnums of all sorts, hydrangeas, from the ten-foot bristly *H. sargentiana* to hybrid lacecaps as blue as the Adriatic, many pieris, camellias of several species lighting up the woods in winter and early spring, the virginal sprays of philadelphus, kalmias, close relatives of the rhododendron, bearing trusses of pink cups—and one inspired planting in which the golden ribbons of witch hazel combined with the mauve of *R. mucronu-latum* to create an unforgettable vignette in the woodland composition.

Up into the branches of these trees and taller shrubs many climbing plants clambered and twined and wreathed themselves about to enamel the green glades above eye level. Wistarias, roses, the brilliant foliage of *Vitis coignetiae*, the white lace-cap trusses of schizophragmas and *Hydrangea petiolaris* wantoned among the boughs and twigs of their host-trees.

A little later a Winter Garden was developed beyond the ponds in the stretch of woodland running down to the banks of the Beaulieu River. It became one of the most charming and sequestered places at Exbury and was as gay in February and March as other areas were in May. Here, guarded by the sentinel Scotch pines, their lower limbs removed to admit light, was shepherded a large mixed flock of shrubs that dared the winter and took "the winds of March with beauty". Prominent among them were witch hazels, camellias of several species, including the wild form of *C. reticulata*, the tree heaths and the floral glories of the winter and early spring cherries. At their feet a hundred thousand daffodils nodded in the grass and the "rathe primrose" glimmered wanly among the fallen leaves.

Even in the Winter Garden, however, rhododendrons took pride of place, and the visitor stepping out on a crisp morning in January or February, with the vegetation crackling beneath his feet and all the trees other than the Scotch pines and silver firs naked above his head, would find both species and hybrids warming the chilly scene with their paint-box cheerfulness. Among the species he would find *R. moupinense*, pallid pink and low-growing; *R. ciliatum*, with fringed white blossoms; *R. eclecteum*, variable in colour but for which an Award of Merit was

12

later won by a deep primrose form when exhibited by Edmund de Rothschild; *R. stewartianum*, likewise variable in colour but which also won the Award of Merit; the rose-purple *R. mucronulatum* and the noble *R. macabeanum* from the romantic mountains of the little state of Manipur.

This collection of wild species Lionel reinforced with quantities of the early-flowering hybrids, adding to their number in course of time some new varieties of his own raising. 'Nobleanum' in its various colour forms was there, of course, with the old 'Lee's Scarlet'. He was particularly fond of 'Red Admiral', which he had had from J. C. Williams, and which he described as a "magnificent blood red, a grand hybrid from Caerhays that never fails to bloom at Exbury in the first week of February and goes on for two months." Another winter favourite was the rose-purple 'Tessa', "that fine cross of Stevenson's between *R.* 'Praecox' and *moupinense*."

These, however, were equalled or surpassed by some of his own raising as they came along and were added to the Winter Garden. Among them were the neat and compact 'Bric-a-brac', resembling its beautiful *leucaspis* parent in its white and rounded flower and opening in the first week of February in a mild year, the red 'Abbot' and 'Alix', both also flowering at that early date, the primrose dwarf 'Bo-peep' and the large, rich-pink 'Amalfi' and 'Androcles'. As their initial letters show, the A's were his very first year's raisings and the B's his second,[1] but all except 'Abbot' won the Award of Merit. Much later still he added to this fine Winter Garden collection his magnificent honey-gold 'Fortune', flowering in spring, on which we shall have more to say.

The list goes on until it looks like the catalogue of the largest nurseryman. But trees and shrubs by no means exhausted Rothschild's enthusiasms. He had a very soft spot for daffodils, of which he raised some hybrids. Primroses were everywhere and bluebells fringed the borders of the woods. Hostas (which Rothschild knew as funkias) thrust up their broad blades and hyacinthine spires. Carpets of cyclamen spread themselves out here and there to peer down at the feet of trees. In a little boggy dell near the large pond primulas and *Phormium tenax*, the New Zealand flax, added variety to the azaleas and Japanese maples. In another small bog near the big rock garden more primulas associated with *Rhododendron hippophaeoides* and the rhubarb-leaved gunneras. Bold clumps of Pfitzer's juniper splayed out their bristly fingers wherever one turned.

Nor was outdoor gardening alone sufficient for this man's enormous energy and catholic sympathies. "Who loves a garden loves a greenhouse too" and in the long ranges of greenhouses, flanked by an herbaceous border 140 yards long, he manifested the wide extent of his affections. In a large tropical house, its air as hot and humid as in a Pacific island jungle, he laid out an indoor garden in which he grew the beautiful small Javanese rhododendrons, together with bananas, the "spring-faced cherubs" of water lilies, oranges, glowing like "golden lamps in a green shade", bougainvilleas and the like, with purple tibouchinas clambering to the roof and hanging down exuberantly.

[1] This practice was not invariable and has not been pursued by E. de R.

In another large house, measuring a hundred by fifty feet, with less heat but similarly laid out as a garden, he planted a collection of tender rhododendron species from sub-tropical regions, the tallest plants nearly reaching the ridge at eighteen feet and their honeyed breath embalming the whole house. Here he had such choice and ambrosial species as *maddenii*, *dalhousiae*, *nuttallii* (true), *lindleyi*, *edgeworthii* and *bullatum* (now sunk under *edgeworthii*). Most of these grew very well and several received awards.[1]

Later this house was used intensively for hybridizing. Plants of various species were lifted from the woodland in autumn and planted in baskets or tubs to be forced into flower at given times. When *R. griersonianum* was all the rage as a parent, Lionel gave orders to have a plant in bloom from early March onwards. The honey-scented *R. discolor* was used similarly, while other species had to be retarded to enable them to be used on the later sorts. Hanger, who later became his head gardener, records: "A telephone message would come from London to gather perhaps a dozen different rhodo blooms with pollen to be ready for Mr Lionel's next week-end visit and before his day's tour of the grounds ended a plant of *R. discolor* in a basket or tub would be married to all those flowers."

The greater part of the greenhouses, however, was devoted to orchids, for which Lionel became almost as famous as for his rhododendrons. Predominantly he cultivated cymbidiums, cattleyas and cypripediums, among other genera. Cymbidiums took pride of place and in this genus he raised many superlative new hybrids which won high awards and which were, after his death, to fetch fantastic prices in the United States. The same was true of nerines, in whose orbicular form and gold-dusted petals he took particular delight and of which he raised some beautiful new cultivars in pink and red. They had their own house to themselves, as also did clivias and hippeastrums, of which, before long, he had assembled the best collections extant.

In yet other houses that flanked these exotics, the discerning visitor in August or September might well have exclaimed with Marvell:

> The luscious clusters of the vine
> Upon my mouth do crush their wine;
> The nectarine and curious peach,
> Into my hands themselves do reach;

---

[1] The First Class Certificate was awarded to:

Forrest 26618, *R. edgeworthii* as *bullatum*. A very fine, tender form, with a much-puckered leaf and an indumentum almost golden-brown, pure white flowers and chocolate anthers.

Forrest 27687, *R. taronense*. A beautiful, round, rather flat flower, with yellow markings at the base of the lobes. Kingdon-Ward 3776, *R. pachypodum*. Large, starry, white flower.

Rock 59557 (never named). An enormous flower, almost identical with the huge trumpets of *R. nuttallii*. *R. rhabdotum*. This had earlier received the AM when exhibited by Bodnant.

The Award of Merit went to:

R. nuttallii var. *stellatum* (KW6333). Smaller blooms than the type with a green calyx.

R. mishmiense, deep yellow.

R. pectinatum.

R. lindleyi, pink form.

R. stenaulum, purplish-rose.

R. auritum.

Indeed, there was scarcely any botanical family of garden importance that this remarkable man did not cultivate, except cacti.

The long recital is not yet complete, however. Lionel had a strong sense of atmosphere and thought the garden incomplete without some animal life. With a sort of poetic justice, in replacement of the pheasants that had been reared as targets for the sportsman's gun, he introduced a quantity of gorgeously plumed, exotic pheasants that roamed the woods without fear of man, finding at Exbury the very shrubs and trees with which some had been familiar in their native haunts.

He made friends with a pair of robins which nested under the elegant branches of 'Naomi' and which perched on his hand to feed from worms that he carried in a tin box. He was very attracted by badgers and had a seat placed in "Badger's Hole" so that he could watch them.

The development of Exbury was not, of course, all achieved at once, but it was achieved remarkably quickly. The astonishing thing is that Lionel de Rothschild had possession of the estate for only twenty years before another war put an end to his activities, with his death following soon afterwards, yet within that span he developed what was incontestably the finest rhododendron garden in the world, adorned with plants that were estimated at a million in number, had become internationally acknowledged as one of the first authorities and had made 1,210 crosses, from among which 462 new varieties were named and registered, far exceeding the performance of any other grower.

Its renown, unlike that of most famous gardens, rested less upon the beauty of its landscaping—though to be sure there were some splendid and moving vistas—than upon the superlative quality of its plants. He uncompromisingly destroyed anything that was second-rate and sought from all over the world not only the best species and varieties but also the finest forms of each. If he learnt that there was a superior specimen of a plant in Scotland, for example, he would send his chauffeur off—a thousand miles there and back—to secure the pollen. For Sir Edmund Loder had already demonstrated, in his renowned 'Loderi', how greatly the progeny of superior forms in the parents could excel those of inferior forms of the same progeny.[1] Of this practice Lionel was a firm disciple.

He personally supervised all major activities and he was to all intents and purposes his own head gardener. Leaving his London offices on Friday and driving his two-seater Rolls-Royce himself, very fast, he would meet his senior gardening staff on arrival, hand each of them a cigar and give his orders for the week-end's operations. He personally determined the positions of all plants of importance, pushing his walking-stick into the ground and saying: "Plant it there." He himself carried out most of the hand-pollinating and, if the selected parents were not ready, gave his head gardener exact instructions on what crosses were to be made during the following week.

His first official head gardener was Fred Kneller, who had been with him at

[1] The old hybrid 'Kewense' had been bred from *griffithianum* × *fortunei*; Loder used the same species, but superior forms, and produced a greatly superior hybrid.

Inchmery. On retirement, Kneller was succeeded by Arthur Bedford, after whom was named one of the best lavender-flowered hardy hybrids ('A. Bedford'), raised by Mr Thomas Lowinsky. Bedford was a fine breed of gardener and his death, when it came a few years later, was deeply felt. Having just returned to Exbury from Chelsea Flower Show, where Lionel de Rothschild, as was his wont, had made a large exhibit, Bedford sat down on a bench, observed "Ah, well, another Chelsea over," and with that utterance died from a sudden thrombosis.

After a short interregnum, in which Jock Findlay was in charge of the woods, Benjamin Hill of the orchids and Francis Hanger of the other greenhouses, Hanger took over as head gardener for the period of the Second World War, after which he became Curator of the Royal Horticultural Society's Garden at Wisley until his death. At Exbury he was succeeded for a short time by Harold Comber and not long afterwards Mr Fred Wynniatt took over at a crucial period. Wynniatt had begun at Exbury as a journeyman gardener in 1938, joined the army after the outbreak of war and returned to Exbury in 1945, when his unbounded industry, quick perceptions and instinct for flowers soon made their mark. He died in 1971 after long service under Mr Peter Barber (co-author of this book), who became agent to Edmund de Rothschild after Lionel's death and later Managing Director of Exbury Gardens. Today, after many years' service, the head gardener is Mr Douglas Betteridge.

Lionel de Rothschild's spectacular achievements inevitably brought him to the forefront of the horticultural universe. He became a stalwart supporter of the Royal Horticultural Society and repeatedly won high awards. He put up splendid exhibits at Chelsea, but the great event of the year was the annual rhododendron show, when he entertained the staffs of all the exhibitors to dinner in their working dress. At Chelsea on one occasion a sudden frost damaged many exhibits in the tents on the day before the opening, but a telephone call to Exbury set the gardeners working nearly all night to dig up the finest shrubs, which left in a convoy of fifteen lorries at 4 a.m., resulting in what was afterwards described as a "staggering" display.

Extending the bounds of his RHS activities, Lionel was one of the founders of the select Garden Club and, more significantly, he founded and became president of the Rhododendron Association (now, alas, no more). Previously there had existed a very small and exclusive Rhododendron Society, of which Lionel had been elected a member in 1920; founded in 1915, it had published annual *Notes*, had initiated the systematic list of rhododendron species and had instituted the annual rhododendron show, but there were only twenty-five members. This was too small and tight a circle, in Lionel's view, for promoting the interests of the rhododendron and on 3 May, 1927, he presided at a meeting at which the new Association was formed.[1] This new organization quickly swelled to a membership

---

[1] The first Council, elected at a meeting two months afterwards, consisted of: Lionel de Rothschild (president), Admiral A. W. Heneage-Vivian (vice-president), J. B. Stevenson (treasurer), J. J. Crosfield, The Marquess of Headfort, G. W. E. Loder, The Hon H. D. McLaren (later Lord Aberconway), Peter Veitch, F. Gomer Waterer, E. H. Wilding and P. D. Williams.

Fig. 4
Floral forms: campanulate or
bell-shaped (*R. dictyotum* 'Kathmandu', AM).

of some 650, including the most illustrious as well as the humblest of the King's subjects, together with many from overseas. The old Society lingered on for several years, with ever dwindling numbers, but was not formally wound up until 1952.

L. de R. himself took on the editorship of the new Association's Year Book and he wrote frequent articles in it which are still full of meat. He wrote on many aspects, including his own remedy for getting rid of rhododendron fly (which is given in Part IV here), but mainly he wrote on hybridizing, suggesting promising matings and warning beginners against others; thus he laid emphasis on the non-compatibility of lepidotes and elepidotes, on the uselessness of putting the pollen of a short-styled rhododendron on the stigma of a long-styled one, on the difficulties of mating azaleas with other rhodos and the different results to be expected when using the tall and the dwarf forms of *R. campylocarpum.*

An even more durable feature of the Association's Year Book, and one for which rhododendron lovers everywhere will always be in debt to Lionel, was the systematic listing of all species and hybrids, which, built up from year to year, developed into what is now the *Rhododendron Handbook*, the indispensable studbook of the genus under the imprint of the RHS.

Another of his activities for the Rhododendron Association was to set aside a part of his garden in 1930 as a trial ground. This was in an open part, exposed to all weathers. Members were invited to send specimens to it and the Committee of the Association visited it regularly to recommend awards to the Council of the Royal Horticultural Society. It was a little slow in showing its value, but some of our most famous hybrids owe their awards to the trials conducted there. The first First Class Certificate went to the blood-red 'Earl of Athlone', from C. B. Van Nes of Holland, in 1933. Other winners that are still in the forefront included Slocock's 'Unique', 'Dairymaid', and 'Souvenir of W. C. Slocock', Waterer, Sons and Crisp's 'Blue Peter', Blaauw's 'Britannia', Koster's 'Betty Wormald' and 'Mrs G. W. Leak', and Knap Hill's 'Mrs Furnivall', to name but a few. In 1938, as Exbury was too remote, the rhododendron trials were transferred to the RHS Garden at Wisley.

Besides all this Lionel gave away thousands of plants, which are now to be found in every country where the Western style of gardening is practised, and did more than any other man to popularize the rhododendron, so that, in its diverse forms, it was soon finding its way not only into the broad acres of the wealthy but also into the smaller gardens of the country at large. "None of his best plants," wrote Aberconway, "did he ever wish to keep to himself; indeed the more widely they were shared the better was he pleased".[1]

He financially contributed at an early date to the plant-hunting expeditions of Forrest and Kingdon-Ward and from the seed they sent back flowered and hybridized the wonderful species that had so long remained hidden from the Western world in the wild mountains and valleys of China, Assam and Upper Burma. His first record of having used this seed is in 1920, when he sowed those from Forrest's 1919 expedition to Upper Burma and the Chinese frontier provinces; from this came many treasures.

His activities and his enormous enterprise brought him the friendship and the wisdom of most of the leading practitioners of the day, whether they were proprietors of great and spectacular estates, such as Lord Aberconway, the Williamses of Cornwall (from whom perhaps he learnt most of all), J. B. Stevenson of Tower Court, Admiral Heneage-Vivian, Major Frederick Stern (as he was then), Sir George Holford, Stephenson Clarke of Borde Hill, or professional specialists such as W. J. Bean, Kingdon-Ward, the plant explorer, and the leading nurserymen of the day. From all he learnt eagerly and rapidly, soon to become a teacher himself. Social standing was of no account and the only passport to his society was a knowledge and love of flowers. In turn, he infected many others with his own passion, including young Ambrose Congreve, nephew of Lady Bessborough.

[1] *Rhododendron Year Book* 1946.

All these and many others he would invite to Exbury for his famous "gardening week-ends", when, enjoying the splendid hospitality of Lionel and his wife, they would tour the woods, holding council on plans for the next stage of development, while their host drank avidly from their common pool of experience. In the evenings he would entertain them with his cinematograph films, in which he mixed his floral sequences with Wild West ones and other excitements. Mr Frank Knight, himself a frequent visitor, speaks nostalgically of the "friendliness of it all and the wonderful spirit" that pervaded Exbury on these occasions. Five motor-cars and chauffeurs were kept at Exbury solely for taking visitors to and from their railway stations.

Other visitors there were besides dedicated gardeners. Winston Churchill came with his cousin the Duke of Marlborough. Winston was bored by horticulture, but he painted in the woods, played bezique and enthralled the company with his brilliant and informed talk. Queen Mary, in whom the love of flowers was strong, came one Cowes Week, arriving by water, and the last plank in the new pier that Lionel was building in the Beaulieu River was being nailed home as she came alongside.

A few years later she came again, this time accompanying King George V, who planted some *Chamaecyparis formosensis* and interceded to save the life of a chestnut that Lionel had marked for destruction. The Prince of Wales (now Duke of Windsor) came, too, and Exbury still sends him consignments of plants nearly every year for the garden of his house near Paris. King George VI, a keen gardener, his queen, Elizabeth, and his sister, Princess Mary, the Princess Royal, came more than once. Indeed, in later days, no one was surprised by the spectacle of Queen Elizabeth and the Princess Royal scrambling among the shrubs to read the plant labels. George VI accepted from Rothschild a quantity of rhododendron hybrids and seedlings, some of which subsequently won high awards under the skilful cultivation of Sir Eric Savill, the Director of the Gardens of Windsor Great Park. Prominent among these were the Jalisco grex, with numerous clones, together with the gay 'Grenadine' and some clones of the celebrated Hawk grex.

The war of 1939 once more brought all gracious things to an end. Once more "the lights had gone out in Europe". Britain, groping her way in the strict blackout, was very soon facing the Axis powers alone. The young men of Exbury went off to the war and with them went Edmund de Rothschild, Lionel's eldest son, who was an officer in a Territorial unit of the Royal Artillery. To his great relief, he escaped the embargo on military service which had so much upset his father in the previous war, and he served until 1946.

There followed some harsh years for Exbury, as for the rest of Britain. Lionel fell ill. Only a skeleton staff was left in the garden and the greenhouses. Exbury House was straddled by bombs on one occasion and the air raids on Southampton

The New Era

violently disturbed the rural peace. The fuel stringency required the shut-down of all the heat in the greenhouses, except for the cymbidium houses, where the material was so valuable that the Ministry of Agriculture gave permission for its continuation (a permission that bore handsome fruit in dollar earnings after the war).

Otherwise, nearly everything in the greenhouses was lost. Gone were the exotic plants in the tropical houses. Gone were the tender and sweet-scented species in the rhododendron house. Gone were tens of thousands of orchids, among them being quantities of seedlings that had excelled all others in existence, being the fruits of Lionel's most mature and experienced breeding. The houses of all those treasures became invaded by the plebeian tomato and cucumber to help feed a hard-pressed nation.

On 27 January 1942, at a moment when the fortunes of the Allies throughout the world were at their very nadir, Lionel died in London at the age of sixty.

The war tended to obscure contemporary recognition of his achievements, yet he had left a rich treasure to the gardens of the world. He had built up a store of floral wealth from which still richer dividends were to be distributed after his death. He had spread a new gospel which has brought the finest of flowering shrubs into the smallest gardens as into the largest. He had increased the knowledge and love of gardens and had brought delight to many people. No memorial has been erected to his memory, but it might be said of Exbury, as it is on Wren's tomb in St Paul's: "If you would seek a monument, look around you".

On the death of his father, Major Edmund de Rothschild, still serving in the army, succeeded. His father had always wanted Exbury to become a home for children evacuated from towns in the bombed areas, but instead the Admiralty had commandeered it shortly before his death. Edmund de Rothschild, hurrying down from Scotland on leave, was given forty-eight hours in which to clear the big house of all its furniture and valuables and on 7 May it became a "stone frigate" under the style first of His Majesty's Ship *Mastodon*, then HMS *King Alfred*, and finally HMS *Hawk*, which, itself commemorating the great admiral, later gave its name to one of Exbury's finest rhododendrons.

So, on the resounding bare boards of Exbury House and in the fleet of huts that were quickly set in array in the elegant grounds, there began in great secrecy the Royal Navy's initial preparations and trials for the Normandy invasion that was to take place in 1944. Next door, Inchmery was taken by the Army (quartering the Free French for a period) and on the water and banks of the Beaulieu River strange and prophetic forms began to assemble where once the ships of Nelson's age had been launched.

Floating Dock No 33 was launched in the river in March 1944. A hundred invasion barges and numerous landing craft were moored, with a maintenance base at Buckler's Hard. At Stanswood, near the mouth of the river, some of the components for the invasion "mulberries" were built. The whole district became a "prohibited area" as, behind a rigid security wall, the planning and the preparations mounted for the invasion of Normandy. Thus, as the months went by, Exbury and all the little creeks that flowed into the Solent became assembly places for the liberation forces.

King George VI came down shortly before D Day to inspect HMS *Hawk*. The captain, knowing well the King's private enthusiasm, quickly mugged up some rhododendron lore, but when the inspection was over and the King went for a walk in the woods, the captain quickly found that the King needed no tutor.

After the Second War, an entirely new prospect, a harsher prospect, faced the young owner of Exbury. Britain had beggared herself for a second time in defence of her integrity. A crushing burden of taxation lay upon the nation and hardest of all upon the wealthy. All over the country splendid and historic houses, among Britain's most beautiful and most renowned heritages, the epitomes of gracious living and instructed taste, full of fine pictures and furniture and surrounded by gardens that were the admiration of the world, were forced one by one to become more or less commercialized and to be formed into limited companies for their means of preservation. Some were made over to the National Trust for England and for Scotland. Others were lost for ever.

Exbury, by careful management, was able in part to sustain the new severities, but the great days of expansion were over. The house, having been handed back by the Admiralty, was not reoccupied. Edmund de Rothschild, with his wife Elizabeth, went back to the home of his infancy at Inchmery. Lionel's arboretum, which had become a forlorn tangle of thorns and tares during the war, was turned back again into farms. The splendid rock garden became a desolation of brambles.

The great rhododendron wood, however, was maintained. If its carefully tended glory was by a little diminished, it gained by the burgeoning of those new species and those new hybrids that Lionel never saw. He never knew the golden splendour of 'Crest', noblest child of the Hawk grex, which he had bred from the pollen of his own 'Lady Bessborough' on the stigma of *R. wardii*, one of his dividends from supporting Kingdon-Ward's explorations. Nor did he ever see the moving and deep-damasked beauty of 'Queen of Hearts' or the dramatic fires of 'Kiev'. He never knew the enormous fame that was to be won by the stunning new dwarf species *R. yakusimanum*, which he had introduced to the Western world and whose story is related in Part II.

To sustain the main gardens, Edmund de Rothschild later found some degree of commercialization inevitable. He did not, however, follow the practice of others in opening their houses to the public, but insisted to his agent that "we must get our living out of the land". Accordingly a new emphasis was given to farming and forestry and part of the 250-acre woodland garden began to be developed, as unobtrusively as possible, into a nursery of fine shrubs. Inevitably rhododendrons predominated, including those superb sunset azaleas for which Exbury is famous and of which a new and even more glittering range has now been developed. A new impetus was given also to the camellia, particularly the varieties of *C. japonica*, which people had begun to realize no longer needed the shelter of great greenhouses, and the cultivation of which is being enormously popularized. Of these developments we shall read later.

Part Two

The Work in the Woods

The Work in the Woods

Like most gardeners, Lionel de Rothschild began his Exbury adventure with limited knowledge. He went through the usual phases of an amateur gardener, but went through them very fast and, having a very quick eye and so much expert advice at hand, passed rapidly from the stage of an apprentice to that of master gardener. Having an imaginative mind to match his prodigious energy, he was no copyist of stereotyped fashions and developed quickly into an innovator.

"To any amateur with a big garden who wishes to start hybridizing," he wrote,[1] "I might perhaps quote my own experience. I was visiting Caerhays for the first time and the owner [J. C. Williams] asked me what crosses I had made; when I told him, to my intense surprise, he told me to burn the lot. Needless to say, I did not follow his advice but, needless to say, also, I have done so since.

"They were made between hybrids of the old Waterer rhododendrons and naturally in nearly every case reverted to the *ponticum*, the mauve colour of which is undoubtedly dominant. He also advised me to study the Mendelian theory and to follow the system that the orchid growers have used with such success.

"He then pointed to some plants growing near and told me that if I picked seeds of those and raised them I should do better, even haphazard, than any I had made. They were primary crosses and I did pick some of the seeds and, while the others are burnt, they are still growing at Exbury."

To the question "Why hybrids?" he replied: "The answer is a very simple one; the species has usually adapted itself to a particular climate, a particular rainfall, a particular resting period when it is covered with snow, even a particular variety of soil in its mountain home. The hybrid, when it is a mixture, is often more able to adapt itself to the vagaries of our climate, nearly always more easily grown in our gardens and, being a hybrid, flowers at an earlier stage and often more freely than the parents."

He cited *R. griffithianum* as a case in point. Its loose bells, he said, were of far greater floral beauty than the tight trusses in vogue in Victorian days, but there were few places in Britain where it could be grown. To introduce its qualities to our climate it had to be crossed with a hardier mate. "No rhododendron," he wrote in 1933, "has had more influence on the beauty of the modern hybrids than this grand species, which, alas, is only seen at its best in the very mildest parts of our country."

The great Loderi grex had already brilliantly proved this point, through the mating of *griffithianum* with the hardy *fortunei*, and Lionel followed suit with his own splendid Angelo grex, with 'Exbury Cornish Cross' and with the Yvonne grex, of which the finest clone ('Yvonne Dawn') has only recently come to light.

Such dicta, however, were the fruits of riper experience. Other sorts of problem faced him when he began his great enterprise at Exbury. A particularly serious one was honey fungus, which spread its black boot-laces insidiously through the ancient woodland soil of the New Forest. It was particularly destructive on the site that he chose for his spectacular rock garden, where he lost a lot

[1] *Year Book* of the Rhododendron Association, 1933.

25

of plants of fine, selected forms. Difficulties of a different sort confronted him from seed sent back by explorers from homes vastly different from Hampshire. He had sown quantities of Forrest's seed as early as 1920 and in 1922 was sowing more of Forrest's and Kingdon-Ward's as well. By studying their field notes and by close conversation with the explorers themselves, he did all he could to provide each species with the conditions that seemed most promising, but he had his failures. "Gardening," he said, "would be too easy if it was always a success."

In rhododendrons (with which we shall henceforth be exclusively concerned) it was unavoidable that he should have started with what was the common stock of the day—the hardy hybrids of the nurseries and such species as were then available from the same sources. It followed that these were the sorts planted nearest to the house, where development began.

In the first year he bought largely from Gomer Waterer, one of his early mentors, from Gill, Veitch, Reuthe, Smith of Guernsey, Harry White of Sunningdale and Van Nes of Holland, and acquired many others "thanks to the generosity," as he acknowledged, "of Captain C. H. Tremayne, of Carelew" (after whom he named a hybrid that was never registered). In the same year he pollinated a plant of *discolor* by a flower of *auriculatum* sent him from Caerhays by J. C. Williams, which in time was to reward him with the splendid white 'Argosy', one of his early successes and still one of the finest late-flowering rhododendrons. He made twenty other crosses also with *discolor* that year.[1]

In the next year we find him planting out quantities from Loder's garden at Leonardslee, from Guernsey and from Holland again; also "many as presents from Caerhays, including a *sinogrande*, which its most generous owner allowed me to dig up when I was on a visit there at Easter and take back in my car to Exbury."[2]

At a later date he acquired large stocks of the brilliant Knap Hill azaleas, which he proceeded to make even more brilliant. In 1926 he acquired most of the collection of Thomas Lowinsky, one of the leading amateurs of the day and a RHS gold medallist, whose fine garden at Tittenhurst, Sunninghill, was celebrated also for some of the rarer forms of conifer, such as the curious pendulous cedars and the very odd weeping wellingtonias, or "ghost trees".

Lionel spent three days at Tittenhurst and was glad to find many good specimens of rhododendron species, including "a very fine form of *griffithianum* which he had got from Gill", as well as the hybrids of the time. There were also some thirty *discolor* crosses and "a prodigious number of Mr Lowinsky's own unnamed hybrids", together with some young plants from Rock's seed.[3] All these he planted on the slight eminence that he named Lowinsky Hill (now Witcher's Wood) where they keep company with a whole legion of his own finest hybrids. When Lowinsky's hybrids had grown on he introduced several of them, including 'Gina', 'Mrs Walter Burns' and 'Pauline', all of which won the Award of Merit. On several occasions he used Lowinsky's unnamed hybrids as material to produce

[1] The Rhododendron Society *Notes*. Vol II
[2] *Idem*.
[3] *Idem*.

his own, as in 'Fancy Free', 'Fantasy', and, after his death, the gorgeous, crimson 'Rouge'. In addition, 'Pauline' gave issue as seed parent to his own gay and delightful 'Grenadine'.

He acquired others from his many garden friends, especially from the Williams cousins, who became what Mrs de Rothschild called his "godfathers" in gardening. Thus from J. C. Williams (among those he specifically mentioned) he obtained the dwarf 'Blue Tit', now to be found in almost every rhododendron garden, another charming but less hardy dwarf in 'Moonstone', the beautiful but slightly tender 'Royal Flush' in pink and orange, and the tall, tree-like 'Red Admiral'.

'Royal Flush' (*cinnabarinum* × *maddenii*) was to prove one of his greatest treasures. All on one day (one assumes from the sequence in his stud-book), quite early in his Exbury days, he made nine matings with forms of 'Royal Flush' (which he called 'Caerhays Pink' and 'Caerhays Yellow') and from these nine emerged the superlative 'Lady Chamberlain' (LR178), 'Lady Rosebery' (LR179) and the more tender 'Lady Berry' (LR186). The other six came to nothing, but it was a rich day's work, for these three soon proved to be among the world's finest woodland rhodos.

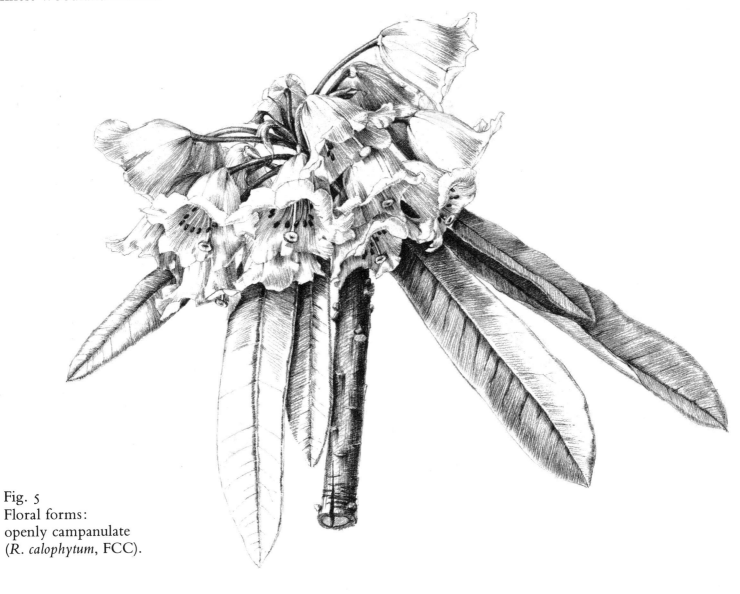

Fig. 5
Floral forms:
openly campanulate
(*R. calophytum*, FCC).

27

From P. D. Williams of Lanarth he had the bright red 'St Keverne', which he used to produce 'Sir Frederick Moore', 'Charlotte de Rothschild' and 'Mary Roxburghe'. From Lord Aberconway he had the beautiful shell-pink 'Cilpinense', the splendid, orange-scarlet 'Fabia', which he called Aberconway's "masterpiece", the brilliant scarlet named after F. C. Puddle (Aberconway's head gardener) and, towards the end, the no less beautiful dwarf 'Elizabeth', with many more of the products of the Aberconways' great garden at Bodnant.[1]

From Alfred Williams, of Launceston, he had the celebrated 'May Day', which he described as a "magnificent scarlet" and thought it better than 'Fabia'. Indeed, there is probably no rhododendron of class that either Lionel or Edmund after him has not introduced into Exbury Gardens.

All the time Lionel was also raising his own new varieties. He freely used all the material that was already available and, more significantly, began sowing the seeds sent back by George Forrest, Kingdon-Ward and Rock, to the problems of which we have earlier referred. The task of growing on the quantities of seed that he had from them was itself immense and slow and the vagaries of the seed were scarcely known.

A trivial act of carelessness showed him the way to easy germination. In 1922 some seed from Kingdon-Ward's and Forrest's collections fell by accident on some "granulated moss litter" that was used for bedding-in the seed pans and this germinated much better than the seed sown in the prepared soil of the pans. Deliberate experiments were made in the next year of sowing in pans of pure peat moss. These were so successful that this method was made the rule.[2]

After they had grown on and flowered, he began his ambitious new programme of hybridization, in which the characteristics of the enchanting styles from the heart of Asia were to give life and light to a long series of new conceptions and to give fresh ornaments to the world. He shared fervently the sentiment of the sonnet that

> From fairest creatures we desire increase,
> That thereby beauty's rose might never die.

These fair creatures had to be wooed, however, with persuasive finesse, if not with passion. Careful selection, skill and patience were the means to success, for it was seven years or so before any results at all were seen and it could be anything up to twenty in the long-leaved sorts.

Perhaps what was most astonishing in his exciting adventures with hybrids, apart from their enormous quantity, was the phenomenal success from his very first year in systematic matings. In due course, these first-year crosses gave him, among many others of good or moderate ratings, the superlative 'Albatross', 'Avalanche', 'Angelo' and 'Argosy'—all in the very front rank of rhododendrons, three of them having *R. discolor* as a parent.

Obviously, he had his failures, however, and the very first entry in his stud-

---

[1] See footnote page 3.
[2] Rhododendron Society *Notes*, Vol II. This method is not now used and has been replaced by the system described in Part IV.

28

book (LR1) was among them. This was *lacteum* × *sutchuenense*, which, after some fifteen years of waiting, proved very disappointing, all the seedlings being discarded. His next three were also failures and the first in his stud-book to become named (though not until 1937) was 'Esperanza' (LR5), one of a group of six *barbatum* crosses. The first in his stud-book to be a real success was LR9, 'Chanticleer', which was to win many prizes with its ardent red bells.

Like other breeders, he had his troubles with *R. lacteum*, finding it reluctant to set seed and sluggish in growth, yet after his death some brilliant successes resulted from his crosses, as in 'Jocelyne', 'Mariloo', 'Lionel's Triumph', 'Repose' and 'Jason'.

As we have seen, he personally determined all the crosses to be made. He watched the results with the closest attention, becoming more critical and selective each year. After germination, he required that every seedling should be grown on to flowering stage, however small or late. "Weeds grow fastest," he would say. Indeed, the celebrated 'Hawk' is said to have come from the smallest seedling in a pan of which he gave the rest away.

Anything that did not then satisfy him, however, went on the bonfire at once. "I shall have a glorious bonfire", he wrote in 1934, "of all my new *cinnabarinum* seedlings", though he had only recently had resounding successes with his magnificent 'Lady Chamberlain' and 'Lady Rosebery'. Much of what satisfied him at first he later knew to be not of the best, though nothing he kept was rubbish.

As his experience ripened he became more and more discerning in his judgement and more exacting in his standards; so that the conceptions of his later years, among which were to be counted some of Exbury's finest products, did not reward him during his lifetime but were introduced by his son, Edmund, and became his legacy to a new generation of gardeners in a more stringent age.

To be a successful hybridist, one must have definite objectives. Rothschild had two: one was to prolong the rhododendron season over as many months as possible; the other, to produce blooms of pure colour. In the first, he obtained a season that lasted from Christmas to the end of August. It began with the old 'Lee's Scarlet', and 'Christmas Cheer', followed soon afterwards by the species and varieties we have noticed in the Winter Garden. Then came all the great company of "the high Midsummer pomps" to, finally, his own 'Leonore' (*auriculatum* × *kyawii*), flowering in August and even into September and accompanied part of the time by J. B. Stevenson's huge, white 'Polar Bear'.

Several of his own raising flowered on into July, when most people thought rather of roses, and among them were the stalwart, tree-like 'Argosy', its snowy mound alleviating the heat of summer, the rich pink 'Norman Shaw' and several of lesser rating, such as the orange 'Felis' and the crimson 'Ironside' and 'Illyria'. Even after the summer was over and before 'Lee's Scarlet' and 'Christmas Cheer' began again, the small, golden, jasmine-like trumpets of 'Yellow Hammer' would occasionally, in advance of their normal season, sound their cheerful fanfares in the late autumn months.

In colour, again like most beginners, Lionel's first inclinations were towards the red shades. His object in breeding in this colour range was to produce a pure red, devoid of any blue infusion. Not that he objected to those that were frankly purple. He was fond of Anthony Waterer's 'Purple Splendour' and would also have enjoyed 'Purple Emperor', which now reigns superbly on the tiny island in the pond, accompanied by one of his own splendid golden azaleas, both dramatically reflected in the water at their feet.

What he disliked, as many rosarians also do, was a red with a blue undertone, which often becomes an overtone as the flower ages. He accordingly began to breed out this infusion and did so with complete success. For this, among other varieties, he repeatedly used 'Moser's Maroon' as soon as it was available, valuing it on three scores—for its hardiness, for prolonging the rhododendron season and for giving profundity of tone in the red sector. Among the red species, he made great use of *kyawii, meddianum, elliottii, eriogynum, thomsonii* and, of course, *griersonianum* repeatedly. From such material he produced splendid cultivars in 'Romany Chal', 'Bibiani', 'Fusilier', 'Kiev', 'Querida', 'Kilimanjaro' and the glorious, deep, dusky-crimson 'Queen of Hearts', perhaps his highest achievement in red, but one that he was never to see. On a totally different level, not characteristic of Exbury at that time, he raised the enchanting dwarf 'Carmen', spreading low and wide and mantled with a profusion of dark red bells.

Besides pure reds, Lionel was eager to achieve pure yellows. He had some good material to work on in the exceptionally fine species *wardii, campylocarpum, lacteum* and occasionally *sinogrande*. From these and their mates, after a modest success in 'Bauble', he produced the impressive 'Fortune', whose enormous trusses moved him to great excitement when they first bloomed, as will later be related. It was the ideal of what a cross should be, being better than either parent and hardier, but it was not wholly yellow, having a magenta splash. 'Idealist', less massive but more decorative, came nearer to the mark soon after his death, and finally came the superb 'Hawk', with all its clonal forms, to delight all who saw its pure sulphur in 1949.

The last cross he ever made also resulted in a very fine yellow. This was *wardii* × *fortunei*, which gave the pure primrose 'Prelude', to win the AM when shown by his son in 1951.

True blue escaped him, as it has done all other raisers, but he collected several specially good forms of *R. augustinii* and planted them in groups which today decorate with their amethystine hues some of the loveliest nooks and glades of Exbury. Continually selecting, he crossed repeatedly with seedling after seedling to get the best colour. J. C. Williams, at Caerhays Castle, was thought to have had a form nearest to pure blue, but not of a high level of hardiness. Lionel, like J. B. Stevenson at Ascot, inter-crossed various forms of the species which had the richest colour with others considered the most hardy, and these are to be found today in some of the finest gardens. Crossing the true species with its smoky-lavender variety *chasmanthum*, Lionel also raised the superlative, deep lavender cultivar 'Electra' and by another cross he raised the tall, amethyst 'Eleanore', a wonderful and generous plant in every way.

Notwithstanding his enthusiasm for pure colour, Lionel also raised many hybrids in pink and blended colours of the very first rank. 'Naomi', 'Carita', 'Lady Chamberlain' in many clonal forms, 'Halcyone', 'Lady Bessborough', 'Bow Bells', 'Brocade' and 'Day Dream' are but a few that head the roll of some of the most decorative rhododendrons in existence. His own favourite was 'Naomi', particularly its form then known as 'Exbury Variety', whose slightly scented flowers were painted in hues of deep cream and rose-opal, but the many other faces of 'Naomi', in diverse soft tints, now formally classified as clones and enumerated in Part III, are scarcely less lovely.

'Naomi' can now be classified as a fully hardy rhododendron and it should be in all but the smallest gardens. In the United States it is rated to resist temperatures down to −15° F. and at Exbury a group stands right out in the open. It never fails to flower, right down to ground level. Lionel used 'Naomi' as a parent also, to result in other varieties, including the altogether delightful 'Carita', 'Idealist' and the new 'Lionel's Triumph', three of the most enchanting rhododendrons in existence.

In addition to his own original work, Lionel de Rothschild frequently made the same crosses as other leading hybridizers, especially where the species *griersonianum* and *griffithianum* were parents. Many of these, as recorded in Part III of this book, won distinction, especially in the greges Matador, May Day, Fabia, Cornish Cross, Calstocker, Red Cap, Isabella and Souldis. Indeed, at least up to 1934, there were few *griersonianum* crosses made by others that he himself had not also made and he recorded that he could not distinguish his own raising of 'Tally Ho' (*griersonianum* × *eriogynum*) from those of Leonardslee and Embley Park.[1]

It must be observed that a great many of these and other hybrids raised at Exbury are by no means of the old "ironclad" order of hardiness. Lionel was, of course, breeding for the embellishment of his own garden, which normally enjoyed a kindly climate, with ample shelter, a slightly humid atmosphere and a plentiful supply of natural water, though, to be sure, it sometimes had bitter enough winters. Gardens all along the west coast, from Cornwall well up into Scotland, provided even more favourable natural conditions with their more plentiful rainfall and more humid airs, though they had their own problem of wind. In such localities and in similar conditions elsewhere in the world, the Exbury hybrids found hospitable homes. Many, however, are given "C" gradings for hardiness (H-4 in the United States; see Part III), but in fact several have shown themselves hardier than in the formal classifications and numbers of the "B" class (in which some shade is recommended for the best results) have proved quite sun-hardy in some situations. 'Naomi', 'Idealist' and the dwarf 'Carmen' are examples. To these has now been added the surprising new purple 'Nicholas', which is of Class "A" hardiness.

In the United States, numerous Exbury rhodos are rated to stand temperatures of below 0° F., a few outstanding examples being 'Naomi', 'Avalanche', 'Crest' (Hawk g.), 'Bow Bells', 'Halcyone' 'Damozel' and 'Albatross'.

Of course, Exbury also grows plenty of the fully hardy "A" class of other

[1] Rhododendron Society Year Book, 1935.

hybridists, including most of the popular "ironclads". Lionel, himself, however, did not long retain great interest in what have been called the "stolid burghers" or, in Sir Thomas Beauchamp's less complimentary term, the "coloured cabbages". Worthy citizens though these are, easy and reliable, they have not the floral distinction, the refinement, the poise and grace of the crosses which the sap of the Asiatic species imparts. He often used a few of them for hybridizing, however.

All the time that he was working in hybrids his affection for the true species remained unabated, for their own sake as well as for their value in hybridizing. He assembled one of the largest collections in existence and the list of awards to species from Exbury, set out here in Part III, is impressive testimony of his love and care and of his keen eye. He not only searched eagerly for their finest forms, but also improved on some of the species by crossing selected parents within each.

We have already shown him doing so in *R. augustinii*. Similarly, he mated the hardiest *R. bullatum*[1] of Rock with the hardiest of the same species from Forrest. Crossing from selected plants likewise produced a very beautiful lemon-coloured form of *R. lutescens*, which was widely acclaimed and won the FCC. He worked also to improve *R. venator*. He had a fine, bright yellow form of *R. wardii*, grown from the Kingdon-Ward expedition to Yunnan in 1921. He was fond of his deep scarlet form of *R. griersonianum*, valuing it for its quick results and for its knack of flowering when very young. He noted "its curious knack of intensifying the scarlet in red rhododendrons and of intensifying the blue in those rhododendrons that have a slight magenta shade in them."

He went on: "For this reason it is but little use crossing *griersonianum* on to the late hardy hybrids such as 'Lady Annette de Trafford' or, in fact, any of the older hybrid rhododendrons which have a shade of mauve or pink; the results always show pink flowers with a distinct tendency to a blue tinge, like some of the old pink phloxes. Crossed with the pure colours, such as 'B. de Bruin' or 'Essex Scarlet', they give excellent results".[2] With these two varieties he himself had some good, though not outstanding, results in such as 'Belisha Beacon', 'Beau Brummell' and 'Mrs Leopold de Rothschild'.

Other species of which he was fond, either for their own sake or as parents, were the lovely white *griffithianum* which gave him 'Angelo' and the fine new series of 'Yvonne', the pale pink, ambrosial *discolor* and *souliei* and the pale mauve *fortunei*. With the striking red tubes of *cinnabarinum* he gave us the unique 'Lady Chamberlain' and 'Lady Rosebery'. *R. lacteum* with *calophytum* as female gave him the magnificent 'Jocelyne' and bequeathed to his son the choice new 'Lionel's Triumph' and 'Mariloo'. He was very fond also of *R. williamsianum*, which is to be seen everywhere at Exbury and which gave him 'Bow Bells', 'Brocade' and his own form of Aberconway's 'Cowslip'. And in his remarkable rock garden, as we shall see later, he grew an enormous number of alpine and dwarf species.

[1] Now swallowed up in *R. edgeworthii*.
[2] Year Book of the Rhododendron Association, 1935.

Fig. 6
The leaf of *R. yakusimanum*,
Exbury form. Left, the upper
surface of the leaf blade. Right,
the leaf cut across in section.

R. yakusimanum

A very particular interest attaches to a small Japanese species which Rothschild introduced into Britain in 1934 which has recently seized the imagination of rhododendron lovers everywhere. This is *R. yakusimanum*, a dwarf of superlative and unique character and in a class quite by itself. Some mysteriousness is attached to its public appearance, of which the actual facts may now be recorded. Before doing so, however, we will consider its character and appearance.

"Yak", as it is often called by those who are on terms of intimacy with it, forms a low, mounded shrub, three feet high, or slightly more, in this country and spreading rather more widely, with its lower branches keeping close company with the ground. Its habit is dense and compact, making it an ideal rhododendron for even the smallest garden and a first-rate inhibitor of weeds.

Its first remarkable feature is its foliage. The leaves, about three and a half inches long by one and a half inches broad, curl downwards and inwards along their margins, so that they appear almost tubular. When young, the leaves and petioles are almost completely covered with a white felt, like those of *Stachys olympica* (*S. lanata*), the popular "Lamb's Ear". Gradually they turn dark green on their curved upper surfaces, while their lower surfaces develop a heavy, woolly indumentum, which is cinnamon in the Exbury form.

Thus in its foliage alone *R. yakusimanum* is a shrub of pronounced ornamental value, but the surprise occasioned by its dramatic young leaves is surpassed by the performance of the flower in May. First there appears a large ball of tightly-packed buds in deep rose-pink. These gradually open to a cluster of some ten bells of paler pink. As they fully expand, the truss becomes completely white, except only for a few faint green spots within, and almost completely spherical, sitting close down on the foliage and of the most elegant deportment.

Apart from these fascinating changes of colour in flower and foliage, the surprising things are the relatively enormous size of the flower trusses in relation to the plant as a whole and the enormous quantity of bloom it bears. It begins to flower when a few inches high and two or three trusses sometimes spring from the same point. The whole plant, with its balanced carriage and faultless habit, bears the imprint of quality and distinction.

Moreover, in spite of its misty mountain origin, it has proved completely sun-hardy as well as frost-hardy in Britain, while in the United States, with an official rating of H-3, it is classified to endure a temperature of -5° F., but in fact has been found by Mr David Leach to be even hardier than that.

R. yakusimanum was found on the small island of Yakushima in the China Sea, 120 miles south of the southern tip of the Japanese mainland. Yakushima is a rain-forest island, consisting almost wholly of three mountains, the highest of which rises to 7,100 feet. It has an exceedingly heavy rainfall and is almost continuously shrouded in mist. Besides "Yak", the island has given us two others described in America as *R. yakusimanum montanum* and the azalea *R. yakuinsulare*, which grows on all the three mountains at 4,000 feet and above.

R. yakusimanum was first formally described by Professor Nakai, a Japanese botanist, in *Trees and Shrubs Indigenous in Japan Proper*. It was placed in the series Ponticum, sub-series Caucasicum—not a category in which one would expect to find a rhododendron of pre-eminent merit and beauty. It is closely related to three other species that share certain of its characteristics—*metternichii*, *degronianum* and *makinoi*. Indeed, the recent *Flora of Japan* classifies it as a variety of *R. metternichii*, but its status as a separate species is elsewhere widely accepted.

In 1934 Lionel de Rothschild wrote to Mr K. Wada, a nurseryman of Numazushi, Japan, who had been a source of many garden treasures, asking him to supply any plants he could of unusual character and high quality. In response, Wada sent him, among other things, two very small plants of *R. yakusimanum* and two or more of the true form of the rare *R. metternichii*. In the same year Rothschild tersely described Yak in the year book of the British Rhododendron Association.

The two small Yaks grew on slowly at Exbury, putting out their white tufts of foliage and their large snowballs each year, but not in a very prominent position and seemingly escaping close notice. After the war, however, one of the two plants was translated to the Royal Horticultural Society's Garden at Wisley.

In 1947 the Wisley plant was exhibited at a RHS show, was acclaimed with a storm of enthusiasm and won an unquestioned First Class Certificate. Three years later the Exbury plant was exhibited at Chelsea by Edmund de Rothschild with an equally devastating effect.

The two plants, which are the largest specimens known in cultivation so far, have slightly different characteristics, but both are of the highest excellence. Mr David Leach, the American authority, tells us that they have quite different genotypes. For serious breeders who may want to make back-crosses or sibling crosses of F1 progeny, a matching of genotypes is very important. The Exbury plant is a trifle more vertical in its carriage and has rather the better foliage, the leaves being doubly convexed and a deeper green. This, according to Dr A. F. Serbin (in the *Quarterly Bulletin* of the American Rhododendron Society of April 1965) is the form found in the higher levels of Yakushima Island, in an area constantly drenched with mist and fiercely windswept. That it should be so superlatively successful in a totally different environment, even enduring exposure to full sun with complete equanimity, is another of its most gratifying surprises.

Still rare, not very cheap and eagerly sought after, *R. yakusimanum* bears promise of becoming a widespread favourite when more generally available, so instant is its appeal both to the connoisseur and to the prentice gardener. It requires some skill, however, to propagate by vegetative methods. From naturally produced seed it varies considerably in its results, for it mates readily with other rhododendrons through the agency of the bee. Inevitably it became eagerly demanded by the hybridist after its first public appearance. Several hybrids have already been created, but none so far shown rivals the charm of the wilding. No doubt worthy offspring will be born in time, but meanwhile Yak is entirely sufficient unto itself. The ECC form is now called 'Koichiro Wada'.

The Azaleas

Of the many categories of rhododendron for which Exbury became famous, the azaleas were far from least. Indeed, "Exbury azalea" has become an accepted term for those luminous, scintillating and often sweetly scented deciduous hybrids which Lionel de Rothschild developed. They stand in the very front rank of his many contributions to horticulture and their radiance adorns today innumerable gardens, small and large, in many quarters of the globe.

The ancestries of nearly all hybrid azaleas, both evergreen and deciduous, have become highly complicated over the past 150 years. The deciduous varieties have fallen into certain groups that are fairly generally recognized (but sometimes less easily distinguished). These are:

The Mollis azaleas, begun by crossing *R. japonicum* (at that time often popularly called Azalea mollis) with *R. molle*, were often erroneously called mollis × sinensis. They have large and handsome trusses of flowers with a strong element of orange in the colour range, flowering in early May, before the leaves appear, with some inclination to tenderness.

The Occidentale azaleas, flowering a fortnight later than the mollis in pastel shades and scented.

The Rustica Flore Pleno azaleas, which are double-flowered forms of the Ghents crossed with *R. japonicum*, blooming May–June.

The Ghent azaleas.

The Knap Hill azaleas.

The Exbury azaleas.

It is the last three that most concern us. In the International Rhododendron Register the Exburys are included in the Knap Hill group, since the same blood (of nine species) flows in both, but Lionel de Rothschild, by ruthless selection and the infusion of new blood, created a very superior strain, with special characteristics of its own.

The Ghent azaleas were originated in 1825 by a Ghent baker named Mortier. The foundation of this strain was made by crosses between the European *R. luteum* (also called Azalea pontica), whose golden, sweetly scented flowers are worth growing for their own sake, and four American species: *viscosum* (the Swamp Azalea), *nudiflorum* (the Pinxterbloom), *calendulaceum* (the Flame Azalea) and the brilliant red *speciosum*. Later the sap of other species was introduced into the strain, including *R. molle* (not to be confused with the *soi-disant* Azalea mollis). The Ghents are characterized by their honeysuckle-like flowers, usually scented, their twiggy habit and rather tall growth. They have excellent garden qualities and are very hardy.

The Knap Hill and Exbury Strains

The first real advance in the Ghents was made by Anthony Waterer, Senior, at his Knap Hill Nursery, near Woking, about 1850. Having begun to combine *R. molle* with *R. calendulaceum* and the Ghents, he proceeded to select seedlings to cross with *R. occidentale, japonicum* and *arborescens* and back again to *R. molle*.

Waterer, followed by his son, Anthony Waterer, Junior, thus produced a race of plants of a scintillating brilliance, a lively and dancing poise, sweet scent and ample hardiness. Their flowers were clustered in large trusses like those of the broad-leaved rhododendrons, their season extended from early May to the end of June and their colours ran through the scales from tender, silvery pinks to fiery reds. They seemed to be the acme of their kind and found their way into many of the great gardens of Western Europe and recently into the United States. They are still very much to be desired.

The younger Waterer was a crusty and eccentric bachelor. Having ample means for his own modest needs, he treated his choicest azaleas as a sort of floral seraglio, hidden from the common gaze. He liked to gloat over them and glory in their being in his collection alone. None but the chosen few were allowed to see them, and of these Lionel de Rothschild became one. When he remarked that this or that plant would look well at Exbury, Waterer replied that he was sorry, but he had marked it to go into his own garden. Lionel, knowing that Waterer's private garden consisted of only a few square yards, in which he grew only a few herbaceous plants and vegetables, but never an azalea, was not taken in. However, Waterer was at length persuaded to part with some of his better seedlings to Exbury and to the two Williamses at Caerhays and Lanarth.

Lionel, as was his wont, at once used his new acquisitions not for themselves alone but with the object of obtaining an even higher standard. Good fortune attended his good judgement, his expansive industry and his boundless means.

As he watched his new seedlings come to flower he saw one that shone out above the rest in a brilliant butter-yellow; broad-petalled, in a large, well-pointed truss, followed in due course by glorious autumn colour. This had already[1] been named 'George Reynolds' by Waterer and in 1936 it won an Award of Merit when shown by Lionel.

Crossing 'George Reynolds' with some of Waterer's unnamed orange seedlings, he produced the brilliant flame 'Hotspur', an azalea which marked a new epoch and which, in fact, won its AM two years before 'George Reynolds'. Not content with the Knap Hills as they were, he then introduced into them the true *R. molle*, which he had grown from Rock's seed, R 59226; for, as he wrote

---

[1] This small point of dubiety is resolved by the writings of L. de R. himself and of Hanger.

afterwards: "Anybody with a plant of *molle* (true) could be certain of success in raising azalea hybrids if he crossed this with any of the large-flowered bright azaleas of commerce."[1]

On this basis he set out on a lavish programme of hybridizing, accompanied by ruthless selection. As each new batch of seedlings flowered, he selected two of the best reds, the best pinks, the best yellows and so on. He went for colour, substance, vigour, size, texture and decorative quality. He then went on to cross his selections, always keeping them in their colour categories. Every single seedling, however slow and small, was planted out, but, as each year another generation flowered, he destroyed all but the chosen few. Thousands of plants thus went on the bonfire every year. He made in all some fifty matings, from which hundreds of thousands of seedlings were raised and flowered.

Thus he produced not a new race but a new strain which showed, for the greater part, a positive all-round improvement on anything that had gone before. Broad-petalled, of great size and substance, balanced and shapely, poised in rhododendron-like trusses yet of sprightly deportment, the range of colours embraces not only the brilliant reds and the brazen oranges but also the tender hues of silvery pink, salmon, rose, apricot, and of course white. All have a luminous and radiant quality, their colours accentuated by the beauty of the young foliage and, when the season is not too hot, they often remain in bloom for a month.

This is not to say, of course, that the azaleas from Knap Hill itself (in which L. de R. acquired a controlling interest) are not also very good indeed, but they have advanced on their own lines by emphasizing vigour, scent and doubling, and by crossings with *R. prunifolium* × *R. occidentale* and with *R. viscosum* and *R. arborescens*. The fine quality of recent Knap Hills shows in varieties like 'Albacore', 'Wryneck', 'Sylphides' and 'Whitethroat'.[2]

The Exbury azaleas stand at an average of about five feet in height. While they look most decorative in the dappled shade of a light and open woodland, they are entirely competent to face the full sun of May. Whatever the situation, they must have plenty of light and, like all rhododendrons, ample moisture at their feet, abhorring hot, dry soils and enjoying a thick mulch of leaves, peat, bracken or the like.

The Register in Part III(B) shows the remarkable range of colours. The celebrated 'Hotspur' alone provides an example. The Award of Merit 'Hotspur' is flame, but there are eight Hotspurs, all uniform in size, shape and habit, but all different in colour. The strength of the strain through inbreeding is now so emphatic that, by careful self-pollination, the seedlings come remarkably true in colour and habit to their parents. As a result, one may now, through the nurseries, buy "Exbury azaleas" simply by colour at less cost than the named varieties, as though they were little more than so many pansies.

---

[1] 1935 Year Book of the Rhododendron Association.
[2] It has been suggested that there are signs of *R. prunifolium* also in Exbury's own 'Royal Lodge', 'Hotspur', 'Knighthood' and others, by reason of their brilliant colourings and lateness, but there is no recorded evidence of this in L. de R.'s stud-book.

The Evergreen Azaleas

In addition to his improvements in the Knap Hill azaleas, Lionel de Rothschild raised a few evergreen or semi-evergreen sorts of great charm. Nearly all were the results of mating the very variable *R. kaempferi* with other species or varieties.

In the *International Register* these have been classified as "Oldhamii Hybrids" on the supposition that they were crosses between *kaempferi* and the fiery red *oldhamii*. This is not so. The Exbury stud-book shows *R. oldhamii* to have resulted in only one cultivar—the well-known 'Bengal Fire'. The others are of quite widely varying lineages. It seems appropriate, therefore, that they should be included in the "Kaempferi Hybrids", to which they bear a general as well as parental resemblance. For our own purposes, however, we may well differentiate them as the "Exbury Kaempferis".

The specific evidence of the stud-book and of plant labels is amplified by L. de R's own article in the Rhododendron Association's Year Book of 1935. There he speaks of crosses "between *kaempferi* and many other of the evergreen species of the Azalea Series" and he specifically mentions matings that can be recognized as having later resulted in 'Sir William Lawrence', 'Louise' and 'Bengal Fire', all of different breedings. His stud-book shows that on several occasions he made crossings with the little-known *R. scabrum*, though only three were registered. We learn from this source, indeed, that he raised a large number of seedlings from all sorts of parents, but only a limited number reached the stage of being named and registered.

Those that came through the test have turned out to be attractive variations on the popular theme of 'Malvatica' × *kaempferi*. Most are fully hardy, several to the extent of an "A" rating, but perhaps none is fully evergreen in the colder counties. Like their relatives, they have an open and airy habit, sometimes growing in elegant tabulations or tiers, and varying in height from three to six feet, with about a four-foot average. With the exception of the delightful, amethystine 'Pippa', all are in various tones of pink, orange-pink or red.

Like the popular dwarf, evergreen Kurumes, but with not the same compact density of foliage, these Exbury Kaempferis become smothered in a tapestry of multitudinous flowers, borne singly or in pairs. Most of these flower late in May and carry on into June to meet the arrival of the roses and thus are of great value in filling what is an awkward floral gap in smaller gardens. Pictorially, they no doubt look most charming in light woodland. They will stand full sun, which helps to ripen their wood against the chills of winter, but the stronger colours are liable to become bleached.

The Exbury azalea story, however, is still not finished. A completely new range of deciduous varieties is being developed which will surpass even the triumphs of Lionel. New breaks in colour, larger flowers and still more intensified brilliance of tone have been produced. As yet unnamed, they are considered by Exbury to be superior to anything of their kind so far.

The Rock Garden

Like other gardeners, Lionel de Rothschild found that the woodland conditions in which he grew the larger genera did not at all suit the alpine rhododendrons, most of which demanded more open situations. But his appetite was omnivorous and he set out to create, as far as he could, a situation that would please them. For this purpose he built an immense rock garden, two or more acres in extent. It was designed to accommodate, among other species, the true alpines that grew at high elevations in the Himalayas and the Chinese alps, which have a wet climate in summer and are enveloped in a protective blanket of snow in winter. The snow was beyond Lionel's means, but he went to the limits of what was possible in the soft but variable climate of southern England. He did not have to count the cost, which was in fact never counted but which was certainly of an astronomical altitude.

The site he selected was adjacent to an old gravel pit deep in the woods, with "a kind of ravine" leading up to an open hollow. On each side of the ravine some oaks gave a certain amount of shade and, where they overhung, of protection from frost. Clarence Elliott, a leading nurseryman and plant-hunter, was commissioned to do the work. Vast quantities of sandstone were brought in from Wales and were skilfully built up into terraces, cliffs and moraines by Mr Edward K. Balls. A water supply was brought in and batteries of fine sprays installed so that every part of the rock garden could be well soaked once a week. In the crevices where *R. forrestii* (then *R. repens*) was to be planted, pipes were sunk behind the stones to enable water to be applied from underground.

As the open hollow was exposed to the east wind, *Pinus radiata* was planted to form a quick-growing shelter belt and mitigate the drying effect of March winds. All round the rock garden a fringe of the Triflorum series was planted, mostly of the willowy, diversely coloured *R. yunnanense*, not only for the floral effect of their butterfly flowers but also because their light and agreeable foliage made a happier companionship for the alpines than the heavy green of the *discolor* hybrids that covered that part of the gardens.

So massive was the scale of operations that it took nearly four years to complete the construction and main planting of the rock garden.

As in other parts of the gardens, the insidious black fingers of honey fungus gave a great deal of trouble. One hundred plants of *R. russatum* that Rothschild had raised from the finest blue form were wiped out. Heavy losses were likewise suffered in the Sanguineum sub-series. Trouble occurred also when a mass of underground springs welled up on one side of the ravine, where the clay of the river valley meets the gravel of the New Forest formation. Not realizing this until heavy rains had occurred, Lionel lost many of his fine lapponicums, but he turned the experience to profit by replanting this area with *R. hippophaeoides*, which enjoys bog-like conditions and which became luxuriant in foliage and flower in its best deep lavender form.

A great deal of what was done was, of course, a matter of trial and error. There

Fig. 7
Floral forms: funnel-shaped,
borne axillary (*R. racemosum*,
FCC).

were plenty of failures as well as successes. Much of value was learnt by experiment. *R. calostrotum* (which Lionel knew as *riparium*) was lost in part by honey fungus and in part by waterlogging. Kingdon-Ward's aromatic *R. fragariflorum*, which carpets the ground with little, crushed-strawberry blossoms, did not care for its seaside altitude but, since it came from 15,000 feet up in the Himalayas, this was scarcely surprising. Many others also gave difficulty, but it was often found, after experience, that a move to a different site brought success. Thus it was learnt that all the lapponicums liked to be right in the open, unshaded. The same was found true of *R. lepidostylum*, whose bright, blue-green young foliage, almost hiding the pale yellow flowers, Lionel found particularly beautiful.

On the other hand, the mauve *R. virgatum* and the pink and bristly *R. scabrifolium* were badly cut by frost and had to be moved to the shelter of trees. The aromatic *R. caesium*, with greenish-yellow bells, which Lionel had grown from Forrest's seed gathered in Yunnan, was also entirely happy under an oak.

These and many other experiences proved valuable lessons for growers of the rarer sorts. But perhaps the most interesting, if the least surprising, was to find how some species enjoyed these conditions far more than the woodland environment. Thus the beautiful milky *R. leucaspis* (which won the FCC and later the AM in a sulphur-tinted form), which braves the chills of February, put out leaves twice its usual size against the sandstone. The scarlet *R. sperabile* var. *weihsiense*, whose natural habits Lionel had learnt from field notes (and for which he secured another AM), had already been growing indifferently in the woodland, but now it thrived, growing twice the size and resisting frost perfectly. The same was true of the white, sweetly scented species then known as *R. bullatum* (another FCC), tender plant though it is, and the shy, ground-hugging *R. aperantum*. The plants of *R. forrestii* that he grew in rock crevices prospered exceedingly, increasing in size of leaf and vigour wherever they touched and crawled over the rocks. In similar crevices, their toes tightly pinched by the rock, but their roots cool and moist beneath it, the pygmy *R. campylogynum* nodded its pretty little purple or pink bells as happily as in its high mountain home of the Himalayas. Exbury had some particularly charming forms of this pixy-like rhododendron, one of which won the AM and the other, when shown by Edmund de Rothschild, the FCC.

As for the easier alpines and other dwarfs, these romped away. *R. keleticum* and *radicans* swarmed over the rock faces; *R. impeditum, russatum, racemosum, scintillans, dasypetalum, flavidum* and *chryseum* surged over the slopes in waves of purple, mauve and yellow.

Alas, the Second World War and the stringencies that followed it brought to an end the glories of Lionel de Rothschild's fabulous rock garden, but see p. 44.

Exbury Today

E xbury still remains a beautiful and very large private garden, a living memorial to its founder and a treasury from which many other gardens of the world have been endowed with many-coloured splendour. It has not the scenic grandeur and the long vistas of Stourhead, Bodnant, Sheffield Park, Muncaster Castle, Windsor Great Park and the lovely coastal gardens of western Scotland, such as Crarae and Inverewe, for it has no commanding elevations and no great expanse of water; it is nevertheless an enchanting woodland scene, in which, as one walks along the paths, great banks of floral opulence crowd in on every side with dappled sunlight filtering in from the guardian trees above, with sudden nooks and glades surprising the beholder as he turns a corner, with now and then a "grex" of gorgeously apparelled pheasants rustling in the deep quilt of fallen leaves.

It is true that, to those who knew Exbury before, its former glory has somewhat diminished in brilliance. It is not as immaculate as it was. The bracken is not quite conquered by the scythe. The old rock garden was designedly abandoned to the brambles and the seedling birches. Here and there the silver firs, as they out-topped the vegetation that formerly protected them, became skeletal ghosts.

Yet, if the polish of Lionel's day has worn off, the patina of nature has in part paid compensation. In its maturity it has taken on the aspect of a natural woodland. The bracken, the brambles and here and there a fallen bough, by partially effacing the hand of man, have given to this corner of King William's forest a new charm. The solitary visitor, quitting the paths and standing amid the silence of the tall oaks, the rufous boles of the Scotch pines, the spreading arms of the magnolias, the massed rhododendrons and azaleas, the heavily berried limbs of the cotoneasters, with the gaultherias spreading underfoot among the fallen leaves, may well imagine himself alone in the primitive grandeur of a woodland made by nature before the arrival of man.

Much, of course, was still kept in good order. The Home Wood, which one enters by the majestic gateway of an ancient Lebanon cedar, the ponds over which the kingfisher flashes and into which a marauding heron occasionally dives, the Main Avenue, where 'Naomi' and 'Bow Bells' flank the approaches to the classic bridge, and Azalea Drive, where the maples and the sumachs challenge the azaleas in their glory of autumn colour, these and other parts were well maintained. Whatever was of horticultural importance received attention. The axe was put to the ghostly silver firs.

Among the innumerable precious things that Lionel de Rothschild left behind are many that have for years been hidden treasures in the woods. The partial neglect of the war years, the encroachments of nature and the break in continuity of ownership and management concealed for many years the whole extent of Lionel de Rothschild's enormous floral legacy. In various parts of the woods many new rhododendrons of the first quality have been found in recent, indeed very recent, years and there may well be still more to be discovered; for it is not only in the desert that flowers "are born to blush unseen".

Two of these were rhododendron species and both, when discovered and exhibited, at once received Awards of Merit. *R. chaetomallum*, in a turkey-red form, was discovered by Mr Wynniatt almost buried beneath the branches of a *ponticum* that had grown larger and larger with the years. This was from the seed of Forrest's 25601, gathered in his 1924–5 expedition, and had been growing for thirty-two years or more before it was rescued and exhibited in 1959.

The second was *R. dictyotum* 'Kathmandu', a hardy plant with beautiful white flowers, crimson-eyed and spotted, with a dense cinnamon indumentum beneath the leaves. This was away on the far limits of the woods and was not found until 1965. Both received awards, as did other finds noted in p. 111 at the end of the Register.

Other discoveries were hybrids of Lionel's mature work which are certain to make their impact in the future. The glistening, dark red 'Querida' was found at the farthest extremity of the Winter Garden, glowing with life and colour. 'Jeritsa', although registered in the year of Lionel's death, was apparently lost sight of until Mr Wynniatt unexpectedly came upon it nine years later beyond that part of the woods where now the nurseries are. The huge, brilliant crimson flowers of 'Rouge' (one of the fruits of the Lowinsky purchase) had never been seen until 1950, when Mrs Lionel de Rothschild, Mr Wynniatt and Mr Ridsdale (gardener to Brigadier Nicholson) were walking through the woods and were arrested by the sight of its opulent trusses; it was looked up at once in the studbook and Mrs Lionel herself named it on the spot. 'Revlon', a superlative *cinnabarinum* hybrid in the 'Lady Chamberlain' tradition, had been growing for many years at the side of the main drive of Exbury House, when suddenly it came into its own in 1957 with an outburst of its polished, carmine trumpets. Indeed, when this book was revised in late 1978, new awards were still being given by the RHS for L. de R. crosses made before his death nearly thirty-seven years earlier.

Possibly more significant, and the most surprising, of any of these was a plant that had been growing unobtrusively for some fourteen years at the back of the estate yard. This bloomed for the first time in 1954, two days before the RHS rhododendron show. Its huge trusses of deep, rich cream, enlivened by the ruddy eye of *R. lacteum* (for all the world as though a bumble bee were sitting in it), were at once seen to be of the highest floral quality and two days later it duly won its award. So highly was it merited that it was named 'Lionel's Triumph'.

The tale of post-war surprises in the woods is far from finished, however. 'Carita' is an enchanting pastel rhododendron which was registered back in 1935. Its group included the beautiful and highly rated clone 'Golden Dream'. A few years ago, however, a new clone in biscuit and rose was discovered. It is now named 'Carita Inchmery' and, in the authors' estimation, is perhaps even more delightful than 'Golden Dream'. Other post-war finds were the purple 'Our Kate' and the piratical 'Bud Flanagan'.

Then, in 1976, came a near disaster, the delayed effects of which are still being experienced. In June came the Great Drought, when the thermometer rose into the 90s and stayed there for most of three months. Large stretches of the English countryside was burnt as brown as a desert. Many of the public reservoirs were emptied and severe water restrictions were imposed by the authorities, who declared that two years of rain would be needed to re-fill the reservoirs. At Exbury the water-table fell nine feet and the roots of plants struggled down and down to keep touch with it.

Worse was to come. The Great Drought (the worst in English meteorological history) was suddenly followed by torrential rains, which lasted through the whole autumn and succeeding winter. The parched reservoirs were filled to overflowing in two months instead of the two years predicted by officials. The rivers ran in spate. In many areas the countryside and many villages were flooded. At Exbury the water-table rose even higher than its normal level and the extended roots of trees and shrubs became water-logged and so "drowned". Thousands of plants were lost, including trees more than 100 feet high. Soon afterwards fungus crept in upon weak plants.

Out of disaster, however, there came some gains, as often happens. The Great Drought and Great Rains of 1976 cleared much of the over-crowding that had been occasioned by neglect due to economic pressures. Nor were all the plants of the highest merit lost. Accordingly, after the enormous task of clearing out all the dead growth, a great re-planting was begun, with new, young stock of Lionel's best creations, as well as chosen ones of "other men's flowers". One result of all these changes is that not all the varieties entered in our Register are to be found today.

New plantings of particular interest to the enthusiast were made and to these have been added seedlings that have developed from L. de R.'s support of botanical explorations. Thus the garden in several parts has become young again. Lionel did not appear to have had any great interest in garden design, but now new vistas have been opened up here and there, inviting the eye of the visitor to

Fig. 8
Floral forms: rotate or
widely funnel-shaped
(*R. davidsonianum*, FCC).

some distant feature. At about the same period the old water installation was discontinued, much of the piping having become corroded, and now the irrigation is by plastic piping fed from Exbury's own reservoir.

A renovation of a more dramatic nature took place recently in one of the least expected parts of Exbury—the once fabulous rock garden. The two or more acres that this ambitious project embraced had become a jungle, but it has now been cleared, at a very large expense of labour though, at the time of writing, it has not yet been planted. It will, we apprehend, be somewhat different from Lionel de Rothschild's conception, which was dominated by dwarf rhododendrons. Certainly we shall see some of these, but there will be plenty of other genera also. Economically it will, no doubt, be somewhat venturesome, but it will vastly increase the attractions of visitors to Exbury. For them it is not very conveniently placed, being to the eastern flank of Azalea Drive, but we do not doubt that it will draw many pilgrims when it has been completed.

This is the romantic face of Exbury. Its other, less apparent to the eye of the visitor, is the commercial. The enormous floral wealth that Lionel left has been developed in several directions by his son. Flowering and berrying shrubs and trees of all sorts besides rhododendrons, but always of the best, chosen forms, are assembled for packing in what used to be the glasshouse for the tropical rhododendrons and sent out far and wide overseas as well as at home. Large exports are made to the United States, where the Rothschild rhododendrons have found great favour and where several, especially 'Naomi', have been found to resist temperatures much lower than those experienced in Britain. Unhappily, all but a very few of the world-famous orchids have been disposed of; so have all the nerines.

In mere numbers, probably azaleas head the lists of Exbury's output. Enormous quantities are raised from seed from Lionel's selected colour strains and the "Exbury azaleas" sold by colour groupings, or as mixed seedlings, are now distributed by every shrub nursery of any standing in addition to the resplendent named cultivars. A still further improved strain, known as the Solent range, has been carefully developed from Exbury's very best, of scintillating (and sometimes brazen) splendour. They are the very latest thing.

Very large quantities of camellias, raised from cuttings by mist propagation, stand on the wide benches and in the frames, their lustrous dark green foliage glistening and growing fast. There has been a tremendous increase in Britain in the growing of camellias, especially the varieties of *C. japonica*, now known to be fully hardy in most parts of Britain, given ample moisture and an acid soil.

In species also the long list of awards goes on. In recent years these have been won by *R. floribundum* 'Swinhoe', in a fuchsia-like colour combination of purple and crimson; the aptly named *R. irroratum* 'Polka Dot'; a beautiful form of *R. pseudochrysanthum* having white bells, crimson in the throat and flushed with divers tones of pink; the white, crimson-splashed *R. wiltonii*, its young shoots clad in a silver-grey felt; the pure white *R. dictyotum* 'Kathmandu' with its suede-like indumentum; the turkey-red form of the fleecy-leaved *R. chaetomallum* and the 'Exbury' clone of *R. coryphaeum*, having white flowers tinted with translucent yellow and a ruby-red throat. More recently still, awards have been won for the old blood-red form of *R. arboreum*, for selected forms of the five-leaved *R. quinquefolium*, the American azalea *R. vaseyi*, the close-knit *R. rigidum* and a form (so far unnamed) of *R. morii*.

The breeding of new cultivars also goes ahead strongly, not so expansively as in the old days, but perhaps with more discrimination gained from the experience of years. So far 154 crosses have been recorded in the new "ER" stud-book. *R. lacteum* has been a particularly successful parent in producing award-winning progeny, among them being 'Galactic', with terrific, pale cream trusses on a strapping plant, the stalwart 'Fred Wynniatt', with flowers of peaches-and-honey, bearing a red streak on each lobe, and the new 'Our Kate', with huge trusses of white flowers flushed with pink and already fifteen feet high at Exbury.

We look forward to seeing very soon some of the latest creations, among which are the strawberry-hued cross between 'Gladys Rilston' and 'Jibouti', which may be called 'Mrs Eddy', and a cross between *R. campylocarpum* and 'Crest', which is a bright yellow and has, so far, a nice compact carriage.

Crosses have inevitably been made with *R. yakusimanum*, but no progeny has yet equalled the quality of the parent by Exbury or any other source. What Exbury is doing is to ally it with some carefully chosen mate and then back-cross it with the FCC form of Yak ('Koichiro Wada'). In the current breeding programme, under the aegis of Edmund de Rothschild, the emphasis is on raising hybrids that have the quality of bloom of Lionel's best, but are hardy enough and of sufficiently moderate stature for everyman's garden. Many of Lionel's best award hybrids are being used: 'Naomi', 'Crest', 'Carita', 'Idealist', 'Kilimanjaro', 'Day Dream' and so on. As one walks round one sees frequently the influence of *R. fortunei*, parent of 'Naomi' and 'Prelude', of *griffithianum* in the purple bloom on petioles and buds, of the burning, incandescent fires of *elliottii* and *eriogynum*, of the gleaming *griersonianum*, so prolific a parent, of the stalwart *discolor*, parent of 'Albatross', 'Lady Bessborough', 'Angelo' and many more— and, indeed, of all the grand galaxy of Asiatic species that, both in themselves and in their offspring, now so sumptuously adorn many gardens of the world.

COLOUR PLATES

1 Exbury House from the entrance to Home Wood

2 Evergreen azaleas near the northern extremity of the woods

3 `Glamour`AM

5 'Idealist' in the shrub

6 'Carita Charm'

1 'Charm'
2 'Golden Dream'
3 'Carita' AM
4 'Inchmery'
5 Unnamed

7 Clonal forms of Carita g.

9 `Tasco`

11 `Persimmon' (Golden Horn g.)

13 'Naomi Nereid' on the balustrade of the bridge

14 An unnamed 'Naomi' at the top of Witcher's Wood

16 A shrub of 'Fortune' FCC in the Winter Garden

17 `Avalanche' FCC in the shrub

19 The Exbury AM form of *Rhododendron pseudochrysanthum*

20 `Bud Flanagan'

21 `Edmund de Rothschild'

23 `Crest' FCC (Hawk g.)

24 Two forms of 'Bow Bells' AM with *Erica x darleyensis*

25 `Hawk' 708 seedling

26 `Mary Roxburghe' (Sir Frederick Moore g.)

30 `Mariloo Eugenie` AM

31 `Exbury Cornish Cross' AM

32 A group of *R. augustinii,* with azalea 'Kirin' and *R. campylocarpum* var. *elatum* in the background

34 `Queen of Hearts' AM

36 `Lady Chamberlain' FCC

37 Indumentum on reverse sides
of various rhododendron leaves

1	Sinogrande	**8**	Arboreum
2	Calophytum	**9**	Bureavii
3	Niveum	**10**	Fictolacteum
4	Fulvum	**11**	Macabeanum
5	Campanulatum	**12**	Campylocarpum
6	Pseudochrysanthum	**13**	Haematodes
7	Yakusimanum	**14**	Cinnabarinum

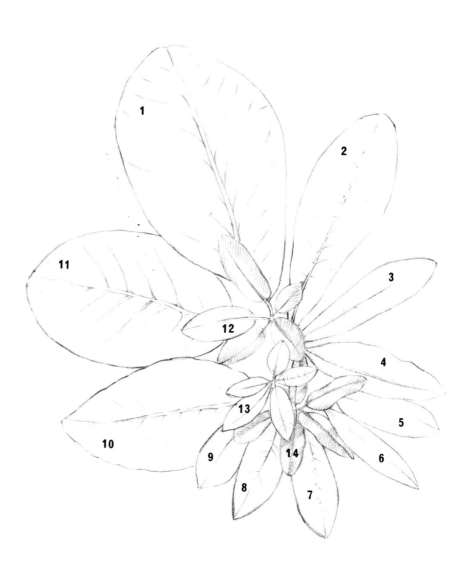

Obverse of the same leaves

39 Azalea 'Scarlet O'Hara'

40 `Citroen', a Solent azalea

41 An unnamed Solent azalea

42 Azalea`Oxydol´

43 Azalea 'Balzac' AM

44 'Beaulieu Manor', a Solent azalea

45 Azalea `Silver Slipper'

46 Azalea 'Ginger'

47 Azalea `George Reynolds' AM

48   Azalea `Hotspur' AM

49 A scene in Azalea Drive

50 `Bastion' (Gibraltar g.)

52 `Perdita' ᴀᴍ (Halcyone g.)

54 `Grenadier' FCC

55 A glade near the top of Home Wood, showing (r. to l.)
'Rosy Morn' AM, 'Dairymaid' AM (Slocock), 'Ivery's Scarlet',
a young 'Day Dream' AM just opening and an
unnamed white clone of 'Loderi' g.

56 `Nicholas'AM

59 `Kiev´AM

60 *Rhododendron fulvum*

61 *Rhododendron yakusimanum* FCC

62 A lakeside scene in the Home Wood

63 Autumn colour by the large pond

1 'Hope' (two blooms)
2 'Exbury Naomi'
3 'Pink Beauty'
4 'Glow'
5 'Carissima'

64 Some of the ''many faces of 'Naomi''''

65 An arrangement of 'Day Dream' AM and 'Exbury Matador' by Mrs Fred Wynniatt in Exbury House

Part Three

The Exbury Register

The Exbury Register

This Register, which in this new edition has been revised up to 1977, constitutes a complete record of all rhododendron hybrids raised at Exbury, including several that are no longer in cultivation there. Exclusive of other raisers' clones, it numbers 491, of which 119 are azaleas. Many have not yet been recorded in the *International Register* or the *Rhododendron Handbook*. In some minor details this Register differs from those authorities, particularly in the evergreen azaleas, in some colour descriptions (most of those given here having been checked with the growing plant), and in the spelling of *R. kyawii* and *R. oldhamii*, in which we have followed the rules of the International Code. The *R. bullatum* of Lionel's time now appears as *R. edgeworthii*. Additions since our first issue are in p. 111 *et sequentia*.

Abbreviations and Symbols

g.   grex   (see page xvii)
cl.   clone   (see page xvii)
ssp.   sub-species (see page xvii)
FCC   First Class Certificate, Royal Horticultural Society
AM   Award of Merit, Royal Horticultural Society
n.i.c.   No longer in cultivation at Exbury

The words "eye", "flash", "patch", etc. are used in this Register instead of the common term "blotch", which, properly used, means a blemish, boil, pimple, etc. (see Oxford Dictionary). In certain instances the eye may well be considered a blemish, in some opinions, but in a great many rhododendrons (as in 'Jocelyne', 'Kilimanjaro', 'Lionel's Triumph', 'Rosy Morn' etc.) it is an adornment and is no doubt always so regarded by the bees.

All clones (where appropriate) are listed under their grex names, but, when the clonal name does not incorporate that of the grex, there is an alphabetical entry for easy reference. Thus there will be an alphabetical entry for 'Crest' under C, but its description will be found under Hawk g.

British and American ratings

Rhododendrons (including azaleas) are assessed by the Royal Horticultural Society and by the American Rhododendron Society for (a) hardiness and (b) garden merit. These assessments are usually good general guides but are approximations only, being based on a consensus of opinion from which individuals may vary. This is particularly so in the United States, where there are great variations of climate and where the northern winters are very severe. The absence of any "official" rating does not necessarily imply that the variety has no value. More often, especially among newer varieties, it means that the variety has not been sufficiently widely distributed for a general opinion to have been formed.

In Britain two systems of assessment are current. Under the newer systems hardiness is expressed by the letter H followed by a numeral, H4 implying completely hardy anywhere in Britain and H1 that the variety can be grown only in a greenhouse. The floral merits of varieties are similarly assessed by the letter F followed by a numeral, F4 being the highest rating and F1 the lowest.

For the purposes of this work, however, the older system of ratings, still current and more generally used, is preferred on various grounds.

British hardiness ratings

Under this system the hardiness of a variety (if yet assessed at all) is indicated by the letters A, B, C, D, E, and F. These apply as follows:

A.   Hardy anywhere and in full exposure in the British Isles and in corresponding climates.

B.   Of equal hardiness to A, but profiting from a little shade to give the best display.

C.   Hardy in the moister counties of the south and west, and in warm, sheltered gardens inland.

D.   Hardy only in the moist climates of the south and west.

E. & F. apply to still more tender categories.

   Under the new system, not here used, H4 is equated to A and B and H3 to C and D.

British merit ratings

Under the older system used here, ratings for ornamental value are shown by stars. Four stars imply outstanding merit, three high merit, two of good quality and one of fair quality.

   Thus a rating of B, ★★ implies that the variety, while frost-hardy, benefits from a little shade and that it is of good garden quality.

American hardiness ratings

   Where any assessments have been made, these are shown by the symbols H–1 to H–7, with a sequence of values that is the opposite of the new British method. Thus:

H–1   Hardy to 25° F. below zero; e.g. in southern New York and south New England.

H–2   Hardy to −15° F.; equivalent to British A.

H–3   Hardy to −5° F.; e.g. in southern Long Island and around Philadelphia. Equivalent to British B.

H–4   Hardy to +5° F. Equivalent to British C.

H–5   Hardy to +15° F.; e.g. in Portland and Seattle areas in most winters. Equivalent to British D.

American merit ratings

Formerly the American Rhododendron Society assigned ratings of x to xxxx, on the same principle as the RHS stars. Under the new system, separate assessments are made for floral merit and for the foliage and growth habit of the plant (on the same principle as the RHS ratings for rhododendron species). These values are expressed by two numerals only, separated by an oblique stroke, in the manner of fractions. The first is for floral quality, the second for the plant, the figure 4 in each case representing the highest value and the figure 1 the lowest, with 2 as average. Thus the rating

H–3, 4/1

implies a variety hardy to −5° F. and of the highest floral merit but of mediocre value as a plant, being leggy or awkward in growth or scant of foliage. This is often useful information on both sides of the Atlantic and elsewhere.

In some instances not all the factors have yet been fully assessed and one or another part of the ratings may be lacking.

Very often American ratings are given only to the grex (usually "group" in the States), implying that there is not yet sufficient experience of the clonal varieties. Occasionally, however, a U.S. rating will be found where none has yet been made by the RHS.

Exbury ratings

Where no RHS assessments for hardiness and merit have yet been made, in most instances the "Exbury ratings" are given. Normally this means that the variety has had little distribution to other gardens, particularly some of the very fine newer sorts, such as 'Lionel's Triumph', 'Nimrod', 'Nicholas', 'Zelia Plume-cocq', 'Mouton Rothschild', 'Jocelyne' and 'Querida', and particularly those of a low hardiness rating, of which 'Kiev', 'Our Kate' and 'Rouge' are conspicuously fine examples. Ten or fifteen years may well elapse, after naming and showing a new plant, before it can be propagated sufficiently for distribution. There are at Exbury some hundreds of rhododendrons that have not been generally distributed, and a good many that never will be, but others there are which, at Exbury, are of very high merit, and of which it will be possible in course of time to make a more broadly based assessment; examples that readily come to mind are 'Janet', 'Oxlip', 'Leo', 'Jeritsa', 'Joanita', 'Jutland' and 'Kilimanjaro'.

It should also be noted that the colour descriptions here are of the cultivars grown at Exbury. In occasional instances, other gardens and nurseries may have slightly different colourings, perhaps through having acquired seedlings not identical with the Exbury clones. Dates of "first reference" are omitted when they are the same as the award date.

Parentage. In quoting the breeding in the following list, the name of the seed parent is given first.

The Register

A. Broad-leaved Rhododendrons

Abalone. g. (*campylocarpum* × *callimorphum*) 1933. One of L. de R.'s very early crosses—LR 31 and 44 in the stud-book. A shrub of moderate size and rounded form. Leaves three inches long, mid-green and glossy above, often slightly recurved marginally, very pale green below. Buds apricot opening to pale primrose, tinted with pink on trusses of moderate size, abundantly borne in some years and then a very attractive shrub, but L. de R. noted that the top buds are apt to be cut by frost in severe winters. April–May.

Exbury ratings: B, ★

Abbot. g. and cl. (*thomsonii* × *delavayi*) 1933. Deep red. Valuable for opening in the first week of February. L. de R. noted that it was "first-rate". In the Winter Garden and only just hardy. LR 32 and 46 in the stud-book.

Exbury ratings: C, ★ ★

Adelaide. g. and cl. AM 1935 ('Aurora' × *thomsonii*). A tall shrub up to twenty feet high, with rounded, dark green leaves. The flowers are wide open bells or bugles, in the blood-red of *R. thomsonii*, slightly freckled within. They have the waxy gleam of the pollen parent and five dark nectar pouches at the base. Quite hardy. April.

British ratings: B, ★ ★

Adjutant. g. (*neriiflorum* × *sperabile*) 1933. Scarlet. L. de R. noted that "it is very free-flowering, covered in bloom, but not as good as either parent." A small and compact shrub, not exceeding five feet. April–May.

Exbury ratings: C, ★

Advie. g. ('Cornubia' × *diphrocalyx*) 1933. Deep rose flowers on a plant of average size and compact habit. April–May.

Exbury ratings: B, ★

Aida. g. ('George Hardy' × *auriculatum*) 1933. White with dark red markings, *n.i.c.*
Akbar. g. and cl. Introduced 1933. AM 1952. ('Loderi King George' × *discolor*) A tall and stalwart shrub of good quality, carrying trusses of twelve florets in deep rose-pink with some crimson streaks in the throat, sweetly scented from its male parent. Valuable for flowering in June.

British ratings: B, ★ ★

Albatross. g. and cl. 1930, AM 1934 (Loderi g. × *discolor*). One of the glories of Exbury and one of the world's most beautiful rhododendrons, this is a very tall, exceptionally fine shrub of the highest rating. Its leaves are long and broad and from them emerge magnificent trusses of flowers of great beauty and distinction, enriched with a honeyed scent. They are deep pink in the bud and open out into immaculate white trumpets, seven-lobed and five inches wide at the mouth, transparently veined, with the reverse of the petals tinted a soft pink. The combination of pink bud and virginal flower is enchanting. The anthers are pale yellow and the style glandular. The shrub flowers with great luxuriance and regularity, is fully hardy and is valuable for carrying the season on into June. Is LR 171 in the stud-book.

British ratings: B, ★ ★ ★ ★
U.S.: (to the grex) H–3, 3/1 (formerly x x x)

Albatross has two fine clones:

> **Exbury Albatross,** FCC 1935. In this very beautiful form the open flowers are a delicate blush pink, with a freckling of mahogany in the throat. It has itself a four-star rating in Britain.

> **Townhill Albatross,** AM 1945. Here the flowers are of fuchsia-pink, paling to white in the centre. From Lord Swaythling's garden.

Alix. g. and cl. Introduced 1930, AM 1935. (*barbatum* × *hookeri*). The brilliant, clear crimson flowers of 'Alix' were said by Francis Hanger to beat all other reds for colour. They are borne with great freedom, but mainly at the top of a tall plant, which is of gaunt habit in the woodland. Leaves rounded. Valuable for opening its flowers in March. In the Winter Garden at Exbury. L. de R. noted that it was "a good red with no blue". Having *hookeri* in the sap, it is only just hardy at Exbury.

Exbury ratings: C, ★ ★

Alpaca. g. Cross made 1926, introduced 1933. ('Sir Charles Lemon' × *neriiflorum*) Pink. *n.i.c.*

Alpine Glow. See under 'Avalanche', of which it is a clone.

Alpine Rose. See likewise under 'Avalanche'.

Amalfi. g. and cl. 1933, AM 1939. ('Cornubia' × *calophytum*). Very early and rather tender, this is a twenty-foot high shrub with mat, green leaves. The funnel flowers are carmine-rose towards the tips of the corolla lobes, shading to white on the tubes, which are freckled dark red with a crimson splash at the base. They are carried in a large, spherical truss. February–March. One of the first pinks to flower in the Winter Garden.

Exbury ratings: D, ★ ★

Androcles. g. and cl. AM 1948 (*arboreum* × *calophytum*). Introduced 1933. A tall but well-knit shrub, following closely the *arboreum* parent. Very large trusses are borne in which may be counted perhaps thirty flowers of rhodamine pink, with four lines of dark spots from the base of the tubes to the ovary. April.

Exbury ratings: C, ★ ★

Amour. A clone of Hawk g.

Angelo. g. and cl. 1933, AM 1935 (*griffithianum* × *discolor*) LR 127 in the studbook, introduced 1930. A splendid, tree-like shrub, which may grow twenty-four feet high, bearing tall trusses of elegant shape and aristocratic character. The flowers are very large, measuring five and a half inches at the bugle-like mouth, seven-lobed, richly scented, blush pink in the bud and opening to pure white stippled with pale green spots within. This green marking is a characteristic of all the clones in this group. Some shade is needed. The leaves are nine inches long and the foliage at all times handsome. May–June.

British ratings: C, ★ ★

U.S.: (to the grex) H–4, 2/1

The Angelo grex includes several good clones and one superlative one:

> **Exbury Angelo,** FCC 1947. Of superb floral quality, the blossoms being white with green markings.   C, ★ ★ ★ ★

> **Sheffield Park Angelo,** AM 1950. Pure white except for a chartreuse patch in the tube base.   C, ★ ★

> **Solent Queen,** AM 1939. Very pale rose, fading to nearly pure white, spotted green within.   C, ★ ★

> **Solent Snow.** White with green markings.

> **Solent Swan.** Pure white.

Annabella. g. (*campanulatum* × Loderi g.) 1933. A fairly compact shrub of average height, with white flowers, flushed mauve. April–May

Exbury ratings: C, ★

Antonio. g. and cl. 1933, AM 1939. ('Gill's Triumph' × *discolor*). A very big plant, tall, wide-spreading and of superior quality. It bears deep rose-pink flowers that wane with age, having a pronounced crimson eye and spotting within, and is sweetly scented. June.

Exbury ratings: C, ★ ★ ★

Antonio Omega is a clone in pale pink,   C, ★ ★

The reputed clone 'Exbury Antonio' is not known at Exbury and must be one and the same as 'Antonio' AM.

Apache. g. ('Gill's Triumph' × *thomsonii*) 1933. Flowers bright rose. *n.i.c.*

Arab. g. and cl. (*williamsianum* × *sperabile*) 1933. This is a shrub of low stature, dense and compact, bearing pink flowers in great abundance in April.

Exbury ratings: C, ★

Argosy. g. (*discolor* × *auriculatum*) 1933. A large, tree-like plant with splendid foliage and large, sweetly scented, white trumpets, with a faint pink flush. Valuable for flowering in June.

Argosy Snow White is a fine, pure white clone, introduced by Waterer, Sons and Crisp, and awarded the AM in 1938.

British ratings: B, ★ ★

U.S.: H–3, 1/2

Ariel. g. (*discolor* × 'Memoir') 1933. A tall but well-furnished shrub, bearing white or pale pink flowers with remarkable freedom in April and May.

Exbury ratings: B, ★

Asteroid. g. ('Dr Stocker' × *thomsonii*) 1933. Of average size and fairly loose habit, with trusses of a rich rose-pink. April.

Two clones were exhibited by Sunningdale Nurseries:

Crimson Banner

Rosy Queen

Exbury ratings: C, ★

Aurora. g. and cl. AM 1922. ('Kewense' × *thomsonii*). A good plant for the large woodland garden, growing to twenty feet or more. The soft-pink flowers are borne in great profusion, are sweetly scented and produce liberal nectar. L. de R. liked it and it deserves particular merit as a parent of 'Naomi' and 'Yvonne'. April–May.

Exbury ratings: C, ★ ★

Avalanche. g. and cl. 1933, FCC 1938, AM 1934. (Loderi g. × *calophytum*). A happily chosen name for a shrub of superlative quality and moving beauty. 'Avalanche' develops into a twenty-foot high dome of stately character, clothed in large, elliptic-oblong leaves. This background, however, becomes almost obscured when the enormous snow-white flowers, twelve or fourteen to a truss, borne on long, rose-red pedicels and enlivened by a small splash of magenta and three lines of colour at the base of the trumpet, cascade to the ground like an avalanche of snow at the end of March, persisting well into April. One is brought up in one's tracks by the spectacle and obliged, like the poet, "to stand and stare".

British ratings: C, ★ ★ ★

U.S.: (to the grex) H–3, 4/3

Two very beautiful clones appear in the Avalanche group:

Alpine Glow. AM 1938. Here the flowers are suffused with a tender but glowing pink and the plant derives its apt name from evocations of sunset on a field of snow.

British ratings: C, ★ ★ ★

Alpine Rose. In this the flowers are of slightly deeper pink than 'Alpine Glow' and of equal merit.

Exbury ratings: C, ★ ★ ★

Avocet. g. (*discolor* × *fortunei*) 1933. A tall, very frost-hardy shrub, growing to a great size, with handsome foliage and scented flowers of mother-of-pearl colourings carried in large trusses. June.

British ratings: B, ★

Ayah. g. (*discolor* × *eriogynum*) 1933. A tall shrub with very large flowers of salmon-pink. June–July.

British ratings: C, ★

U.S.: H–3, 0/1

Ayesha. g. (*discolor* × *arboreum*). Cross made 1926, introduced 1933. A shrub that may reach fifteen feet in shade, but remains compact and well furnished with the rough foliage that it inherits from *arboreum*. The flowers are very bright pink, borne in great quantity and look like a pink waterfall in early May.

Exbury ratings: C, ★

Aztec. g. (*arboreum* × *irroratum*). Cross made in 1926, introduced 1933. Very like 'Ayesha' both in general character and in the colour, but the blooms have a maroon spotting within. It flowers with tremendous abandon at the end of April.

Exbury ratings: C, ★ ★

Banshee. g. (*auriculatum* × 'John Tremayne') 1934. A tall, well-filled shrub with flowers of blush-pink. June.

Exbury ratings: C, ★

Barbara. g. (*campylocarpum* var. *elatum* × Loderi g.). The cross was made in 1934 by L. de R. but not introduced till 1948 by E. de R. A shrub of moderate size and loose growth, bearing loose trusses of unusually lovely deep cream flowers with a soft pink flush, not unlike 'Penjerrick'. "Many shades of colour and a good truss," in L. de R.'s words. April–May.

The clone **Pinafore** is white, veined pink and flushed with pink towards the margins—a charming effect.

British ratings: B, ★ ★

U.S.: H–5, 2/1

Barbet. g. (*dichroanthum* × *callimorphum*) 1934. Creamy pink. *n.i.c.*

Baron Philippe de Rothschild. g. and cl. ('Exbury Naomi' × 'Crest') 1963. A handsome new shrub with the upright and compact habit of 'Naomi', bearing well-formed trusses of large, pale yellow flowers and clothed with becoming foliage. It flowers in profusion and is proving able to withstand low temperatures in a very exposed position. May.

Exbury ratings: B, ★ ★ ★

Bastion. A clone of Gibraltar g.

Bauble. g. ('Dawn's Delight' × *campylocarpum*) 1934. A dense shrub with handsome, small, rounded and glossy leaves and small, straw-yellow bells with lemon styles and filaments. Apt to be shy when young. April-May.

Exbury ratings: B, ★ ★

B.B.C. g. ('The Don' × *neriiflorum* ssp. *euchaites*) 1934. A shrub of normal size and build, with foliage closely following the parent *euchaites* and having red flowers. April. *n.i.c.*

Beau Brummell. g. and cl. 1934, AM 1938. ('Essex Scarlet' × *eriogynum*). A good, late-flowering shrub yielding large, gleaming trusses of some thirty tubular flowers in polished, waxy scarlet with a freckled throat and characterized by black anthers. A colourful and distinctive shrub, of neat and close habit, with pointed, grey-green leaves and a brown indumentum, valuable for flowering in June.

> British ratings: B, ★★
> U.S.: H–4, 2/3

Beaulieu Hawk. A pale yellow clone of the Hawk grex (q.v.).

Belisha Beacon. g. ('Essex Scarlet' × *arboreum*) 1934. Of medium height, having dusky scarlet flowers with a deeper throat, in tight trusses. A trustworthy plant of good behaviour. L. de R. observed: "Good habit, brilliant red in May."

> British ratings: B, ★★

Belle. A clone of Lady Bessborough g.

Bellerophon. g. ('Norman Shaw' × *eriogynum*) 1934. This well-clothed, late-flowering shrub grows to about ten feet with a tidy habit and bears well-knit trusses of ten or more blooms of bright crimson with great freedom. June-July.

> Exbury ratings: B, ★★

Belvedere. cl. of Berryrose g. Soft apricot-pink tones. *n.i.c.*

Berryrose. g. and cl. AM 1934, cross made 1927. ('Doncaster' × *dichroanthum*). A low-growing shrub with large, very attractive, scented, pink flowers with a yellow flare, giving an overall effect of orange. April–May.

> There is also Lord Digby's clone **Minterne Berryrose.** See also the azalea 'Berryrose' and see above for 'Belvedere'.

> British ratings: B, ★
> U.S.: —, 3/3

Berylline. g. (*spinuliferum* × *valentinianum*) 1934. A neat, dense shrub of low stature, bearing very showy flowers of pale gold flushed with rose, in small, compact trusses, with the greatest freedom. April–May.

> Exbury ratings: C, ★

Bibiani. g. and cl. AM 1934 ('Moser's Maroon' × *arboreum*). A hardy shrub of neat and orderly behaviour, growing to twelve feet, with long, narrow strap-like leaves of dark green. As might be expected, the flowers are a rich crimson to dark crimson with a few maroon spots. L. de R. called it "very dark, clear crimson, very constant." Very free-flowering in part-shade. April–May.

> British ratings: B, ★★
> U.S.: H–5, 2/3

Biskra. g. and cl. Introduced 1934, AM 1940. (*cinnabarinum* var. *roylei* × *ambiguum*). An erect and slender bush of up to fifteen feet, bearing very distinctive trumpets of vermilion blended with biscuit, in tight clusters of eight, elegantly

Fig. 9
Floral forms: funnel–campanulate
(*R. fulvum*, AM).

pendant. Usually it flowers with exceptional profusion. The smooth, dark green, elliptic leaves, two and a half inches long, are covered with minute, crimson, resin-bearing cells beneath. April.

British ratings: C, ★
U.S.: H–4, 1/1

Blanc-mange. g. and cl. 1934, AM 1947. ('Godesberg' × *auriculatum*). A good, pure white hybrid with open, funnel-shaped flowers, frilled at the margins and made up in a shapely, well-poised truss of up to eighteen blossoms. The shrub grows fifteen to twenty feet high and of equal spread, with mat, green leaves nine by four inches. May–June.

The clone **Swan Lake** is also white.

Exbury ratings: B, ★ ★

Blushing Bride. g. ('Dawn's Delight' × *discolor*) 1934. Rose-crimson, bell-mouthed flowers. *n.i.c.*

Boadicea. g. (*thomsonii* × *hookeri*) 1934. A tall, upright but compact plant, with bright, waxy, crimson flowers that proclaim their female parent. Very free-flowering and useful for a March display.

Exbury ratings: B, ★

Bobolink. g. (*discolor* × *neriiflorum*) 1934. A compact, medium-sized shrub with deep yellow to apricot flowers. Very free-flowering. May–June.

Exbury ratings: B, ★
U.S.: H–3, 2/2

Bodnant Yellow. A clone of Lady Chamberlain g.

Bonbon. g. (*souliei* × *maximum*). The cross was made in 1927 and introduced in 1934. A compact shrub of middle stature with trusses of cream flowers, generously borne. May.

Exbury ratings: B, ★

Bonito. g. and cl., AM 1934. (*discolor* × 'Luscombei'). This very good hybrid grows to about fifteen feet at Exbury. It is fully hardy, grows fast and has an open habit, with handsome greyish-green leaves composed in bold rosettes. It carries fine trusses of very large individual flowers, which (in the true Exbury form) are white with a chocolate eye, loosely and graciously arranged and sweetly scented. A very reliable, all-round plant. May–June.

British ratings: B, ★ ★ ★
U.S.: H–3, 3/3

Bo–peep. g. and cl. Introduced 1934, AM 1937. (*lutescens* × *moupinense*). This was one of L. de R.'s Winter Garden favourites. The parentage almost guarantees a progeny of refinement and charm, though not of partiality to dry atmospheres. It builds up into a small, pretty bush of about three to four feet, its young, narrow leaves daintily clothed in brown before turning a rich, glossy green. At the end of March it blooms profusely with small flowers that L. de R. described as of "pale primrose", freckled with a deeper yellow, resembling the beauty of *lutescens*. Excellent for seaboard rock gardens and borders. In less genial climates some protection for the buds is advisable.

British ratings: C, ★ ★ ★
U.S.: H–4, 2/2

Bordeaux. cl. (*gymnocarpum* × *beanianum*) 1963. A new rhododendron, first registered as 'Burgundian'. It will not exceed five feet and preserves a compact shape, with small, deep green, glossy foliage, clothed beneath with a brown indumentum. The flowers are dark red and of a waxen, polished texture, appearing in April.

Exbury ratings: C, ★ ★

Bow Bells. g. and cl. 1934, AM 1935. ('Corona' × *williamsianum*). A delightful rhododendron rarely exceeding six feet, compact in habit, with the young shoots bright copper and the mature leaves dark green above, pale beneath. It flowers profusely. The trusses are of airy and graceful deportment, deep cerise in the bud, opening to shapely, expanded bells of a lively pink, paler towards the lobes when fully open. Highly esteemed in the United States. April–May.

British ratings: B, ★ ★
U.S.: H–3, 4/4

Break of Day. g. and cl. 1934, AM 1936. ('Dawn's Delight' × *dichroanthum*). Another low-growing and meritorious shrub of compact habit, good for small gardens. The funnel flowers are in rich sunrise shades, deep orange at the base and flame at the lobes, unusual in a broad-leaved rhodo, and are characterized by elongated, orange calyces. Up to fourteen florets are displayed in open, uncrowded trusses. May.

British ratings: B, ★ ★

U.S.: H–3, 1/1

Brenda. g. and cl. ('J. A. Agnew' × *griersonianum*) 1927. A plant of middle stature and good habit, bearing compact pink trusses. *n.i.c.*

Bric–a–brac. g. and cl. AM 1945, introduced 1934. (*leucaspis* × *moupinense*). L. de R. described this as "a neat, small bush, compact, resembling *leucaspis* in the round flower." This beautiful early rhododendron (maybe too early for cold counties), grows with an open and stylish habit, no more than three feet high, and regularly produces a cascade of the daintiest flowers, which are very widely expanded and pure white except for some faint markings on the upper petal, and are adorned with chocolate anthers like those of *leucaspis*. The bud scales are brightly coloured and persistent. The plant is quite hardy, but in ungenial climates the buds may be frosted unless protected. In the Winter Garden at Exbury. March.

British ratings: C, ★ ★

U.S.: H–5, 2/2

Brigadier. g. and cl. ('Dawn's Delight' × *arboreum*) 1934. Large, close, pink trusses are borne with great freedom on a tall plant of loose habit. April–May.

Exbury ratings: C, ★

Bright Eyes. g. (*griffithianum* × *diphrocalyx*) 1934. White flushed pink. *n.i.c.*

Brinco. cl. (Loderi g. × *thomsonii*). Raised 1928, registered 1955. Following the male parent, this is a tall, erect plant. It carries on this structure big trusses of large individual blossoms which are a bright rose-pink. April.

Exbury ratings: B, ★ ★

Brocade. g. ('Vervaeniana' × *williamsianum*) 1934. This seemingly odd cross between an Indian azalea and a *thomsonii* series resulted in a most attractive rhododendron of rounded silhouette and modest stature, seldom exceeding five feet, and growing with an open habit. The flowers, arranged in graceful clusters, are vivid carmine in the bud and open to frilly, peach-pink bells, elegantly displayed on slightly drooping branches and produced in April–May.

British ratings: B, ★ ★

U.S.: H–4, 2/3

Bud Flanagan. cl. (? × *ponticum*) 1966. A chance hybrid found flowering for the first time in Witcher's Wood in 1962. This plant is now (1966) about four and a half feet high, compact and shapely, with *ponticum* very marked in the foliage and stems; it may ultimately grow to about fourteen feet. It carries enormous, conical trusses of eighteen to twenty large, closely packed florets, which are a lively, sparkling mauve emphasized by a large and spreading flash of very deep chestnut. The whole truss has a bold and almost piratical air and the plant is bone-hardy but may not be to everyone's taste. May–June.

Exbury ratings: A, ★ ★

Bulbul. g. and cl. 1934, AM 1949 (*edgeworthii* × *moupinense*). A rather straggly plant, somewhat tender, with flowers usually in pairs, which, mainly inherited from the female parent, are white with faint yellow markings and chocolate anthers on long stamens. April.

Exbury ratings: D, ★ ★

Burgundian. See 'Bordeaux'.

Burning Bush. g. (*haematodes* × *dichroanthum*) 1934. A low, spreading bush to about four feet, displaying brilliant tangerine bells which are very showy when the plant is in full flower. To obtain the pollen for this cross, L. de R. made a special journey to Harry White at Sunningdale Nurseries, where there was a superior form of *R. dichroanthum*. May.

British ratings: B, ★

Bustard. g. (*auriculatum* × 'Penjerrick') 1934. A tall, very late-flowering plant well furnished with the long auricled leaves of the *auriculatum* parent and carrying a generous load of good, compact trusses of large, pure white flowers. July.

Exbury ratings: C, ★ ★

Caliban ('Doncaster' × *haematodes*). Raised 1925, introduced 1935. Red. *n.i.c.*

Cara Mia. g. and cl. ('Aurora' × 'Crest'). 1966, AM 3 May 1966. The last in this Register to be named and awarded, this is a new rhododendron of great beauty with openly campanulate, recurved blossoms that are pale rose in the bud, opening to a paler rose, shading to deep cream and marked by a small, crimson flash in the throat, the whole floret suffused with a glow as of peaches and honey. The florets are borne on green pedicels from cream calyces with elongated lobes in trusses of twelve to fifteen on a shrub that will attain sixteen feet. April–May.

Exbury ratings: B, ★ ★ ★

Carex. g. and cl. AM 1932, (*irroratum* × *fargesii*). A tall, pyramidal, early-flowering rhododendron of excellent quality, carrying moderate-sized trusses of up to eight blossoms in great abundance. The flowers are a rich pink within, darker without. The leaves, resembling *R. fargesii*, are a soft grey-green. One of the best earlies.

There are two good clones: **Carex Blush** and **Carex White,** whose names proclaim their colours. March–April.

British ratings: C, ★ ★
U.S.: H–4, 3/2

Carita. g. and cl. Introduced 1935, AM 1945. ('Naomi' × *campylocarpum*). This was one of Lionel's happiest and most inspired matings. A first-class hardy species married to his own choicest creation at that time resulted in an enchanting progeny, which is particularly esteemed in the United States. 'Carita' builds up into a bush twelve to fifteen feet high, of rather open and columnar form, well proportioned, graceful in bearing, amply clothed with elegant leaves of rich green on pink stalks.

About the third week of April this bush becomes studded with a mass of mushroom-pink buds, borne on plum-coloured stalks. As the buds open at the end of April, the whole splendid structure becomes completely obscured in a festival of pale primrose which cascades right down to the ground, giving the plant the appearance of being bathed in sunlight. It is fully hardy in Britain and, although classed as a "B", some plants at Exbury grow fully in the open.

A slight tendency to gappiness in the truss bars 'Carita' from highest honours as an exhibition flower, but it is a garden plant of exceptional beauty when well grown. Note the American ratings.

> British ratings: B, ★ ★
>
> U.S.: (the grex) H–4, 4/4

Three clones equal or excel 'Carita' in beauty. They are:

> **Carita Charm.** Deep pink in the bud, opening to cream, flushed and overlaid deep peach-pink. Ten to twelve florets in a beautiful truss.
>
> > Exbury ratings: B, ★ ★
>
> **Carita Inchmery.** The flowers of this clone are of a tender and moving beauty. Deep rose-red in the bud, they open to a warm blend of biscuit and salmon, with a distant overall effect of fawn pink, after which they wane to tints of opal; the whole making a gay and aptly spring-like combination, which marries well with primroses at their feet or contrasts equally charmingly with scillas, muscari and the like.
>
> > British ratings: B, ★ ★
> >
> > Authors' dissent: B, ★ ★ ★
>
> **Golden Dream.** This very beautiful variation on the theme of 'Carita' is sufficiently described by its name, the whole plant being completely mantled in a golden shroud after the opening of its dusky pink buds.
>
> > British ratings: B, ★ ★ ★

Carmen. g. (*sanguineum* ssp. *didymum* × *forrestii* var. *repens*) 1935. Many marriages have been made between the best dwarf form of Forrest's prostrate red rhododendron and other species or varieties. This is deemed the best of its kind. 'Carmen' is a perfect dwarf, suitable equally for the rock garden or the open border, seldom growing more than two feet or so high but spreading widely and neatly with dense, small foliage and smothered with waxy, glistening, dark red bells at the end of April and in early May. Sunshine inspires it with particular enchantment.

'Carmen' associates happily with a wide range of other plants, clothing the naked legs of certain roses, giving shade to the roots of lilies and blending well with heathers; it is indeed, a perfect plant for almost anywhere in the smallest garden as for the largest. It is fully hardy in the British Isles in suitable soils and, *pace* the official rating, has no objection to being fully exposed to the sun, but may not there sustain its floral display quite so long as with a little shade.

> British ratings: B, ★ ★ ★
>
> Authors' dissent: A, ★ ★ ★
>
> U.S.: H–3, 3/3

Castle of Mey. cl. 1963. (*barbatum*, pink form × *chaetomallum*). A new shrub named after the Queen Mother's Scottish home on the occasion of her last visit to Exbury. It is a medium-sized plant of bushy and compact disposition, with a slight fawn indumentum beneath mat leaves of pale green. The flowers are deep red, waxen and shining, bell-shaped, with a double calyx. They are borne in a medium-sized, flat-topped truss. April–May.

Exbury ratings: C, ★ ★

Chaffinch. g. ('Countess of Haddington' × *ciliatum*) 1935. A low-growing shrub of open habit, with neat, mat, hairy foliage, and embellished with small trusses of sweetly scented, pale pink flowers of moderate size, profusely borne. April.

Exbury ratings: C, ★

Chanticleer. g. (*thomsonii* × *eriogynum*). 1935. An excellent hybrid of tall, erect habit, flowering very freely in compact, well-balanced trusses made up of large, bright red, glistening blossoms. 'Chanticleer' is an example of a good marriage and it has won many times in *thomsonii* class competitions. April–May.

Exbury ratings: B, ★ ★ ★
U.S.: H–5, 3/1

Charites. g. and cl. 1965 ('Carita' × 'Crest'). A new shrub of much promise bred from first-class parents, both of which show up well in their progeny. It has an upright and compact manner of growth with smooth foliage of mid-green, and carries well-built trusses of large, open-mouthed flowers of a good, firm, pale yellow. It stands up well to an exposed position in the garden. Sometimes wrongly spelt 'Charitas'. April–May.

Exbury ratings: B, ★ ★ ★

Charles Michael. A clone of Major g.
Charlotte Rothschild. A clone of Sir Frederick Moore g.
Charmian. g. ('Vervaeniana' × *callimorphum*) 1935. Rose and pale pink. *n.i.c.*
Château Lafite. cl. 1963. ('Impi' × 'Jutland'). Another welcome recruit to the ranks of rhododendrons well suited to the smaller garden. It will scarcely attain five feet, with a similar spread. Clothed in deep green foliage, it bears very dark red bells in a truss of medium size. May–June.

Exbury ratings: B, ★ ★

Chelsea. A clone of Lady Chamberlain g.
Clarice of Langau. (*sanguineum* ssp. *didymum* × *haematodes*) 1966. A promising new hybrid for the rock and small garden. Low growing, very compact, with an ultimate height of three to four feet and similar spread. The leaf formation and habit are in a neat, dense and rounded manner similar to *haematodes*, also showing the fawn indumentum of *haematodes*. The dark red flowers are neatly held in a fairly loose truss. May–June.

Exbury ratings: B, ★ ★ ★

Clove. g. (*sperabile* × *sanguineum* ssp. *haemaleum*) 1935. A semi-dwarf rhodo-dendron growing to about four feet with a close-knit habit and bearing very deep crimson bells. April–May.

Exbury ratings: C, ★

Cowbell. g. (*ciliatum* × *edgeworthii*) 1935. This pretty, small rhododendron grows to only about four feet, with a low, spreading habit and hairy leaves. The flowers are pale pink, arranged in loose trusses. April–May.

Exbury ratings: C, ★

Cremorne. g. and cl. 1935, AM 1947. ('Luscombei' × *campylocarpum*). A shrub of good proportions and moderate stature. It flowers very freely in moderate-sized trusses made up of blossoms that change from rose to soft yellow, giving an overall effect of peaches-and-cream. It is perhaps surpassed by Lord Swaythling's clone—

> **Townhill Cremorne,** in which the flowers, twelve to a truss, are soft pink in the bud, dispersing to a soft yellow as they expand, and flushed and margined with coral-rose. April–May.

> Exbury ratings: B, ★

Crest. A clone of Hawk g.

Crimson Banner. A clone of Asteroid g.

Damozel. g. and cl. 1936, AM 1948. (A. W. bright rose × *griersonianum*). This is a branching shrub, usually spreading rather widely and thinly clad with narrow, dark green leaves that are coated with a thin, brown indumentum beneath. The funnel flowers are individually of great beauty and produced in great abundance. They are a deep ruby with darker spotting scattered internally and white glandular hairs, so that they appear as a blend of several suffused tints. They build up as they expand to a shapely dome, having up to seventeen blooms in the truss. Very hardy. May–June.

> British ratings: B, ★ ★
> U.S.: H–3, 3/1

Day Dream. g. and cl. 1936, AM. 1940. ('Lady Bessborough' × *griersonianum*). One of the most beautiful rhododendrons though not fully hardy. It grows into a rather tall plant of open habit, with pointed leaves of a soft, rich green, four and a half inches long and narrowly elliptic. The flowers are arranged in a truss seven inches wide with an airy elegance, not overcrowded, up to thirteen to a truss, and are of most charming colourings. The long pointed buds are a rich rose-crimson and open to widely campanulate flowers (three and a half inches at the mouth) which are of the same shade but which gradually become biscuit-yellow, lit up with a large and glowing rose-red eye. This high festival of colour 'Day Dream' celebrates in the season May–June. It does well in full sun if liberally watered.

> British ratings: C, ★ ★ ★
> U.S.: H–4, 3/2

Devagilla. g. (*discolor* × 'Cornubia'). 1936. A tall but compact plant with rose-pink flowers in good trusses. May.

> Exbury ratings: B, ★

Devaluation. g. (*auriculatum* × *arboreum*) 1936. Likewise tall but compact. The truss is made of individually large flowers that are white with a pink flush. June.

> Exbury ratings: C, ★

Diogenes. g. ('Red Argenteum' × *calophytum*). 1936. A large plant of well-knit habit, carrying very heavy trusses of creamy-pink bells with a deep red patch, having *calophytum* dominant both in the long leaves and the flower. April.

> Exbury ratings: C, ★

Diva. g. and cl. 1936, AM 1937 ('Ladybird' × *griersonianum*). Of commanding habit, this shrub shows *griersonianum* dominant in the foliage, with brown indumentum. The medium-sized, spherical trusses have wide-open funnels of a deep pink, near to red, speckled brown within. Very free-flowering. June.

British ratings: C, ★

U.S.: H–3, 2/1

Dollar Princess. g. and cl. ('Sir Frederick Moore' × 'Tally Ho') 1966. A new rhododendron, growing tall and upright with fairly dark green foliage and promising to be a large shrub eventually. The flowers are of a deep carmine-pink with a glistening texture, composed in a well-built truss. June.

Exbury ratings: C, ★★

Dolly. g. ('Dawn's Delight' × *griersonianum*) 1940. The shrub grows to eight or ten feet with an open habit. The somewhat drooping trusses are a rich pink, flushed cherry-red externally. May.

Exbury ratings: B, ★

Dorcas. g. ('Bagshot Ruby' × *discolor*) 1936. This cross resulted in a tall plant bearing trusses of moderate size composed of rose-pink blossoms, slightly scented. May.

Exbury ratings: B, ★

Dragonfly. g. (*auriculatum* × *facetum*) 1936. This late-flowering shrub grows into a very large, dense plant, massed with handsome leaves, which are long, narrow and rather hairy. From this spring trusses of huge flowers that resemble *auriculatum*, but are carmine. June.

British ratings: C, ★

Drum Major. g. (*arboreum* × *griersonianum*) 1936. A shrub of moderate vigour and fairly open habit, having compact trusses of bright red. April–May.

Exbury ratings: C, ★

Dulcibella. g. ('Diphole Pink' × *eriogynum*) 1936. Bright, rich pink. *n.i.c.*

Dunlin. g. ('Dawn's Delight' × *thomsonii*) 1936. Rose-red. *n.i.c.*

Dusky Maid. g. ('Moser's Maroon' × *discolor*) 1936. As might be expected, this is a tall, erect, showy plant of good quality and robust character. The maternal influence shows strongly in the well-knit truss of dark red flowers. 'Dusky Maid' is one of the parents of 'Kilimanjaro' FCC. June.

British ratings: B, ★★

Easter Egg. g. (*fulgens* × *neriiflorum*) 1937. Blood-red. *n.i.c.*

Edmund de Rothschild. cl. ('Kilimanjaro' FCC × 'Fusilier' FCC) 1963. This fine new rhododendron builds up into a strong, vigorous shrub that may reach fifteen feet, of open growth, with deep, dark green foliage, influenced by 'Kilimanjaro'. It becomes embellished with magnificent, well-built trusses of the deep red, unstained by blue, that Lionel would have delighted in, had he lived to see it. The blossoms are formed in wide-mouthed trumpets, taking mainly after 'Kilimanjaro' in their boldness and true, deep red. A valuable woodland shrub for carrying the season well into June. See also p. 112.

Exbury ratings: C, ★★★

Fig. 10
Floral forms: widely
funnel-shaped and zygomorphic
(*R*. 'Eleanore', AM).

Eleanore. g. and cl. AM 1943. (*desquamatum* × *augustinii*). Introduced 1937. This Triflorum hybrid is one of the beauties of Exbury. The tall, strapping shrub, growing fifteen to twenty feet, but of good habit and deportment, is profusely arrayed with flowers that are a blend of violet and amethyst borne in clusters of four or five. It forms an arresting picture in April and May and is quite hardy. There is also a lavender form.

> British ratings: C, ★ ★
> Authors' dissent: B, ★ ★
> U.S.: H–3, 3/3

Electra. cl. 1937, AM 1940. (*augustinii* var. *chasmanthum* × *augustinii*). A vivid and magnificent rhododendron produced by L. de R. in his experiments in blue. Though, like others, he never realized a true blue in his *augustinii* selections and matings, he produced in 'Electra' a plant of superlative quality and rich floral excellence. The tall and vigorous framework, fifteen to twenty feet high, is well clothed with foliage, the leaves being two and a half inches long and narrowly elliptic. The plant is completely mantled with flowers which are blended of violet and lavender, dappled with chartreuse at the base of the upper lobe, and borne in clusters of up to seven blossoms. In an evening light the colour effect is magnificent. 'Electra' is sometimes said to be difficult to start, but, once established, it flowers luxuriantly. April–May.

Technically, 'Electra' must now be classed as a clone of *R. augustinii*, not as a separate grex.

British ratings: C, ★ ★ ★
U.S.: H–4, 4/3

Elizabeth de Rothschild. g. and cl. AM 1965. ('Lionel's Triumph' × 'Exbury Naomi'). Named after Edmund de Rothschild's wife, this is a really outstanding new cultivar of splendid bearing and classic quality. The shrub, furnished with dark green leaves, six and a half inches long, that show both parents well, is robust, well balanced and well branched, and may reach twenty feet. The big, funnel-shaped flowers measure four and a half inches at the mouth, and are of a deep cream pigment enlivened with chestnut spotting in the throat and displayed in a large, round, well-knit truss of some eighteen florets. Pictorially 'Elizabeth de Rothschild' seems to call for a woodland setting, though fully hardy. May–June.

Exbury ratings: B, ★ ★ ★ ★

Emmeline. g. ('Essex Scarlet' × *haematodes*) 1937. Red. *n.i.c.*

Empire Day. A clone of Romany Chai g.

Endeavour. g. (*arboreum* forma *album* × *lacteum*) 1937. An early-flowering shrub growing with erect habit to fifteen feet, well furnished. The flowers are of deep cream flushed primrose and are borne in compact trusses. March–April.

Exbury ratings: C, ★

Endymion. g. ('Lord Milner' × *hookeri*) 1937. Rich red. *n.i.c.*

Ernestine. g. (*yunnanense* as *chartophyllum* × *cinnabarinum* var. *roylei*) 1937. Of tall but compact bearing, this shrub shows the *cinnabarinum* influence in its bluish foliage and in its waxy, pendant, pink trumpets, which it bears in profusion. April–May.

Exbury ratings: C, ★ ★

Esmeralda. g. ('Loderi King George' × *neriiflorum*) 1937. Pale pink to deep rose. Not of great merit.

Esperanza. g. (*barbatum* × *strigillosum*). The first entry in the stud-book (LR5) to be named and registered, though not until 1937. Of tall, loose habit, with trusses of deep red flowers in the tubular-campanulate fashion of the male parent. March–April.

Exbury ratings: C, ★

Esterel. g. (*arboreum* forma *album* × *meddianum*) 1937. A shrub of moderate dimensions, with well-formed trusses of rose-pink, waxy flowers. April.

Exbury ratings: C, ★

Ethelred. g. ('Gill's Crimson' × *neriiflorum*) 1937. Crimson. *n.i.c.*

Ethyl. g. (*campylocarpum* × *orbiculare*) 1937. This cross of two first-rate hardy species might have been expected to produce some outstanding progeny. 'Ethyl' did not fulfil such expectations, yet is a nice shrub of moderate stature and good proportions following *orbiculare* in its foliage and carrying flowers of cream flushed with pink. April.

Exbury ratings: B, ★

Etna. A clone of Lady Rosebery g.

Euphrosyne. g. and cl. AM 1923. (*arboreum* × Loderi g.) Bright carmine flowers speckled with crimson spots. 'Euphrosyne Ruby' was a clone exhibited by Sir Edmund Loder. April–May.

Exbury ratings: C, ★

Eureka. g. and cl. 1937, AM 1939. (*arboreum* × *hookeri*). This shrub is of moderate dimensions and compact form. The trusses are composed of fifteen to eighteen narrow funnel-shaped flowers, coloured blood-red and stippled dark brown within. April.

Exbury ratings: C, ★

Eurydice. g. and cl. AM 1939. (*arboreum* forma *album* × Loderi g.) A shrub of moderate size, amply clothed and carrying very attractive flowers which are large and funnel-shaped, white with a delicate flush of rose and splashed with crimson within. April.

Exbury ratings: C, ★ ★

Exburiense. g. (*sanguineum* ssp. *didymum* × *kyawii*) 1937. A very late-flowering shrub, being one that L. de R. raised to prolong the rhododendron season. It is of loose spreading habit, with decorative and very dark green leaves, rather hairy, and waxy, bell-like flowers in very dark red. July–August.

British ratings: C, ★ ★

Exbury Calstocker. cl. AM 1948. (*calophytum* × 'Dr Stocker') (Calstocker g.) The cross was first made by Mr Whitaker, of Pylewell Park, and introduced in 1935. The same cross was made later by L. de. R. and gained the AM. This cultivar is distinguished by very large, domed trusses carrying anything up to twenty-three white bells, which are marked with a maroon patch on the upper petals. May.

Exbury ratings: B, ★ ★
U.S.: (to the grex)–, 3/4

Exbury Cornish Cross. cl. AM 1935. (*thomsonii* × *griffithianum*). (Cornish Cross g.) This cross was first made by S. Smith and produced a plant bearing rose-pink flowers. The same parents were crossed again by Llewelyn, producing large and handsome crimson-to-red flowers, to which the AM was awarded in 1911. Later L. de R. also made the same cross, using a *thomsonii* from Sunningdale Nursery and the FCC form of the male (which he called *R. aucklandii*). This resulted in a large, robust plant of loose and open habit, bearing brilliant and exceptionally beautiful flowers which are a deep crimson in the bud, opening to show variations in the depth of colour, their floral distinction emphasized by a patina of soft bloom on the exterior and by small, dark nectar pouches at the base within. March–April. LR 107 in the stud-book.

British ratings: C, ★ ★ ★
U.S.: (to the grex) H–4, 3/2

Exbury Fabia. cl. (*dichroanthum* × *griersonianum*) (Fabia g.) The original cross was made by the late Lord Aberconway and gained the AM in 1934 for its brilliant flowers, in which scarlet, orange and salmon were blended together. L. de R.'s cross resulted in a loosely spreading plant, six to eight feet high, with leaves of a mat, deep green, felted with a tawny indumentum beneath and producing very handsome flowers of apricot flushed with pink, which are the largest flowers of all the several Fabias. May–June.

British ratings: B, ★ ★ ★
U.S.: (to the grex) H–4, 2/2

Exbury Isabella. cl. 1948 (*griffithianum* × *auriculatum*) (Isabella g.) 'Isabella' was raised by Sir Edmund Loder and introduced in 1934; its flowers were a clear pink. L. de R.'s crossing of the same parents resulted in a tall, dense plant with large, white, sweetly scented blooms, flowering June–July.

Exbury ratings: C, ★ ★
U.S.: (to the grex) H–4, 2/2

Exbury Matador. cl. (*griersonianum* × *strigillosum*) (Matador g.) The original 'Matador', to which the FCC was awarded, was another of the fine hybrids raised by Lord Aberconway, having flowers of deep orange-red. L. de R., by the same cross, produced a rather loose and open shrub clothed with dark green leaves, having a buff indumentum beneath and decorated with wide-open flowers of a brilliant scarlet, inclined to follow the seed parent rather than the pollen in style. April–May.

British ratings: C, ★ ★ ★ ★
U.S.: (to the grex) H–5, 2/2

Exbury May Day. cl. (*haematodes* × *griersonianum*) (May Day g.) This superb rhododendron forms a well-proportioned shrub of moderate dimensions, suitable for all but the smallest gardens where the climate is not unfavourable. Its mat, green leaves are coated beneath with a pale buff indumentum and its flowers are a brilliant and glowing scarlet, elegantly displayed in diffuse trusses and borne with great freedom. Very reliable and of superlative quality. All May Days are good. The original, introduced by A. M. Williams in 1932 and awarded the AM, had cerise flowers. Aberconway produced another in 1939 in deeper scarlet. May.

British ratings: C, ★ ★ ★ ★
U.S.: (to the grex) H–4, 3/4

Exbury Merlin. cl. See under Hawk grex.

Exbury Red Cap. cl. (*sanguineum* ssp. *didymum* × *eriogynum*) (Red Cap g.) Introduced by J. B. Stevenson in 1935, 'Red Cap' is a dwarfish and compact shrub with trusses of blood-red flowers. The Exbury variation by the same cross is deep crimson. Valuable for small gardens and for late flowering in June.

British ratings: C, ★ ★ ★
U.S.: (to the grex) H–4, 2/2

Exbury Souldis. cl. 1948 (*souliei* × *discolor*) (Souldis g.) A tall but compact and well-clothed shrub with most attractive flowers. Pink in the bud, they open out into widely expanded funnels or bowls, with white, notched petals and a crimson patch within. The original 'Souldis' was introduced by Magor in 1927, but his plant bore blush-pink flowers fading to off-white. May.

British ratings: B, ★ ★ ★

Exbury Spinulosum. cl. AM 1948. (*spinuliferum* × *racemosum*) (Spinulosum g.) This unusual rhododendron is a rather loosely growing plant. The flowers, borne in clusters rather than trusses, are small tubes, only an inch long and half an inch wide, in colour red flushed orange, with the stamens protruding from the petals, as in the male parent. The narrow leaves, three inches long, are a glossy, dark green overlaid with bronze in the centre and the midrib is brown and scaly beneath. April.

The original 'Spinulosum', of apricot pink, was exhibited by the Royal Botanic Gardens, Kew, in 1926 but not awarded the AM until 1944.

Exbury ratings: C, ★ ★

Fairy Light. g. ('Lady Mar' × *griersonianum*) 1948. A neat shrub of modest dimensions and of fast growth, bearing well-knit trusses of bright pink. A cheerful and reliable plant of good all-round qualities. April–May.

British ratings: B, ★

Fancy Free. g. and cl. AM 1938. (Lowinsky hybrid × *eriogynum*). A compact shrub of moderate proportions, bearing brightly hued flowers that are pink, blended with salmon and speckled darker within. May–June.

Exbury ratings: C, ★

Fandango. g. ('Britannia' × *haematodes*) 1938. This marriage of a popular, bright crimson, hardy hybrid with a first-class species of glistening scarlet has resulted in a hardy and reliable offspring that is very suitable for the smaller garden. Semi-dwarf and well-knit in habit, it bears waxy, gleaming bells of deep crimson-scarlet in May.

British ratings: B, ★ ★

Fantasy. g. (Lowinsky hybrid × *griersonianum*) 1938. A shrub of medium vigour and loose habit with trusses of a full pink. May.

Exbury ratings: C, ★

Farall. A clone of Romany Chal. g.

Felis. g. (*dichroanthum* × *facetum*) 1938. Of low, spreading habit, this shrub has trusses of loosely-knit bells of a gay colour that shades from orange to yellow. June.

British ratings: C, ★

Fez. g. ('King George' × *sanguineum* ssp. *haemaleum*) 1938. Another low shrub of compact and leafy habit, with waxy, crimson flowers borne in loose trusses. April–May.

Exbury ratings: C, ★

Fire Bird. g. ('Norman Shaw' × *griersonianum*) 1938. A tall, very vigorous but well-knit shrub, brightly arrayed with wide-open flowers of a glowing salmon-red. Very decorative and showy. May–June.

British ratings: B, ★ ★
U.S.: H–4, 2/2

Firedrake. g. ('Sardis' × *kyawii*) 1938. Good, showy trusses of bright red flowers which are individually large are displayed on a large but compact shrub. June.

Exbury ratings: C, ★

Firefly. g. ('Crossbill' × *spinuliferum*) 1938. A very attractive and gay shrub when in full flower. Moderately sized and of open habit, it carries trusses of small flowers varying in tone from apricot to yellow, that sparkle gaily in the woodland. April–May.

Exbury ratings: B, ★ ★

Flashlight. g. (*callimorphum* × *campylocarpum*) 1938. A very pretty and generous-hearted rhododendron. The plant is of neat habit, spreading somewhat and growing slowly to perhaps seven feet. The floral sequence is delightful. The buds are vivid orange but open to clusters of bells that are a blend of apricot and lemon, waning to straw-yellow and illuminated with a bright red flash. They are produced with such liberality that they form gleaming cascades in April and May.

Exbury ratings: B, ★ ★ ★

Fortune. g. and cl. FCC 1938. (*falconeri* × *sinogrande*). This was one of Lionel's great achievements and its first flowering gave him a feeling of keen exhilaration. The pollen came from a particularly good form of *sinogrande* owned by Captain George Johnstone, of Trewithen, one of his gardening friends.

Promising to become of enormous stature, 'Fortune' is a plant of majestic bearing. Its large globes of luminous blooms, its strapping, leathery leaves, its robust framework of branches present an image of strength and dominance. As all hybrids should ideally be, it surpasses both its parents, eminent though they are, in its combination of their vital qualities. The young leaves wear a delicate, glaucous bloom and in the second year extend themselves to a full sixteen inches in a dark green habit, but lightly felted beneath with a fawn indumentum from *falconeri*. The well-knit floral globe stands nine inches high and is composed of anything up to twenty-five large Canterbury bells of primrose, richer than those of *sinogrande* and ornamented with a small, crimson patch in the throat, and a large, green stigma exserted.

Mrs Lionel Rothschild has recorded the first appearance of 'Fortune' in 1938. "It was," she wrote, "a lovely April day when Exbury had donned its Riviera look. As we walked into the woods we saw this magnificent plant holding up its glorious blooms to a deep blue sky. In the evening Lionel gathered his family to a round-table conference to discuss the merits of the new seedling. There it stood in the largest vase available, looking most majestic. Not only was the flower outstanding, but its stance and bearing were bold and commanding. Its great leaves were disposed so as to remind me of the Discobolus, the Greek thrower of the discus with arm stretched out and poised for the throw."

A group of 'Fortune' stands today in a clearing in the Winter Garden. For that kind of situation—in any garden of the west or south coastal areas and in any sheltered but well watered garden inland—it is a noble plant, its great globes lighting up the scene like lamps. It flowers in April and May and does so with great regularity and sometimes with abandon. Except for hardiness, it enjoys the highest ratings in both Britain and America. 'Fortune' is not easy to propagate and Exbury itself has only five plants of the FCC form.

British ratings: C, ★ ★ ★ ★
U.S.: H–4, 4/4

Francis Hanger. g. and cl. 1942, AM 1950. (*dichroanthum* × 'Isabella'). This is a very decorative variety that builds up into a plant of moderate size, well clothed with foliage. It bears flat-topped, loose trusses of about seven large blossoms which are of most attractive colouring, being deep yellow, flushed at the margins with pale rose, somewhat in the manner of the rose 'Peace'. Its fault is that the new growth breaks out at the same time as the flowers, which are thus partially obscured. June.

Exbury ratings: B, ★ ★
U.S.: H–3, 2/2

Fred Wynniatt. g. and cl. AM 1963. (*fortunei* × 'Jalisco'). A splendid new rhododendron named in tribute to Major Edmund de Rothschild's head gardener. The plant is tall but of compact and orderly habit. Its flowers, furnished with large, petaloid calyces up to an inch long, are openly campanulate and maize-yellow, the petals margined with a flush of neyron-rose, and are carried in large, flat-topped trusses of up to ten blossoms—a charming and delicate combination. May–June.

The Fred Wynniatt grex has given rise to several meritorious new clones, which were exhibited at the Chelsea Flower Show of 1966. They are:

Jerez. Pale lemon-yellow and of excellent quality.

Joyful. Deep cream, flushed carmine-pink on the outer lobes and with a distinct red line running down the centre of each lobe on the outside and showing pink inside.

Simita. Maize, with a brown eye and slight brown spotting. Of much promise.

Trianon. Rose-pink with golden throat. Of very good quality.

Exbury ratings: B, ★ ★ ★

Fusilier. g. and cl. FCC 1942, AM 1938. (*elliottii* × *griersonianum*). This rhododendron, though not of the first degree of hardiness, has a brilliant and dashing quality. One of the products of L. de R.'s search for a pure red, it grows tall, with a loose and open habit best fitted to a semi-woodland site, and is embellished with large trusses of brilliant red bells, opening three inches wide at the mouth and sprinkled all over within the petals with spots of darker red. The young leaves are handsomely dressed in a brown indumentum as they emerge. A bold and commanding plant that lights up the woodland scene. The FCC form was shown by Lieut-Colonel E. Bolitho, of Penzance. May.

Exbury ratings: B, ★ ★ ★
U.S.: H–4, 3/2

Galactic. g. and cl. AM 1964. ('Avalanche' × *lacteum*). A very fine new rhododendron and a top-ranking collector's plant. Of tall and splendid bearing, it is clothed with foliage that shows *lacteum* very clearly. The flowers disclose the influence of both parents; they are of fleshy texture, in colour deep cream with a small crimson eye, and slightly scented. 'Galactic' flowers with great freedom in enormous trusses of about twenty-two florets and the blooms are resistant to spring frosts. The season is March–April. Award raised to FCC 1970.

Exbury ratings: C, ★★★★

Fig. 11
Floral forms: tubular
campanulate in a tight truss
(*R. barbatum*, AM).

Galloper Light. cl. AM 1927. This is an azaleodendron, the most desirable of such hybrids and much hardier than the equally beautiful 'Glory of Littleworth'. The flowers are rose-pink in the bud, opening to deep salmon and gradually changing to yellow, with a pink flush lingering. They are assembled in a truss of good form, well poised above deciduous green foliage (the weakest feature of azaleodendrons), on a plant attaining about seven feet. May.

British ratings: B, ★ ★
U.S.: H–3, 2/1

Gaul. g. and cl. AM 1939. ('Shilsonii' × *elliottii*). For gardens that can provide the right conditions, we have here a superior and highly decorative shrub. Of moderate build and compact structure, it produces brilliant trusses of some twenty narrow funnels dyed a deep red, a welcome variation on a well-known theme and not so well known as it deserves to be. Hanger remarked that the flowers have "a fine substance and are hard to beat for colour." They have a cup-shaped calyx of the same red. April–May. The clone—

> **Gaul Mastodon** is of a richer red.

Exbury ratings: C, ★ ★ ★
U.S.: H–4, 4/2

Gay Gordon. cl. ('Beau Brummell' × *elliottii*) 1939. A very free-flowering plant of loose habit and medium stature, with a full truss of waxy, shining, scarlet blossoms. May.

Exbury ratings: C, ★ ★

Geisha. g. ('Pineapple' × *dichroanthum*). Cross made 1932, introduced 1939. Of low, spreading habit with cream flowers borne in rather loose trusses. May.

Exbury ratings: C, ★

General Sir John du Cane. g. (*thomsonii* × *discolor*) 1933. Named after one of the leading soldiers of the First World War. A tall and stalwart plant with good, large, rather lax trusses of rose-pink flowers with a dark eye and a sweet scent. One of which L. de R. was fond. May–June.

British ratings: B, ★

Gibraltar. g. ('Bibiani' × *elliottii*) 1939. Another *elliottii* cross of good quality showing itself in large, fringed, deep red flowers of brilliant tones carried in a truss of average size. The plant is of a tall and loose-growing habit suitable for woodland. It has very attractive leaves, which are bright chestnut when young, deep green when mature. Rothschild also raised an azalea of the same name. May–June.

Exbury ratings: C, ★ ★ ★

There is a handsome clone, new in 1961—

> **Bastion.** The flowers are a darker red, with the black spotting of 'Bibiani'. See also 'Red Rock', p. 113.

Exbury ratings: C, ★ ★ ★

Gipsy King. g. and cl. ('King George' × *haematodes*) 1939. A good rhododendron which, in the woodland conditions of Exbury, grows with a somewhat loose and spreading habit, bearing an open truss of red, waxy flowers in April and May. There is a clone—

Memory (not recorded in the *Register* or *Handbook*), awarded the AM in 1945. This has openly campanulate flowers of high quality of a rich, dark red, self-coloured throughout, with the puckered calyx of *haematodes*, and is now being used at Exbury for breeding.

Exbury ratings: B, ★ ★ ★

Glamour. g. and cl. AM 1946, introduced 1939. ('Margaret' × *griersonianum*). A shrub of low and spreading propensities, bearing elegantly formed trusses of ten widely expanded flowers of a deep cherry-red with undertones of orange, expanding to four inches wide. It flowers very freely and is very gay and colourful. April–May.

British ratings: C, ★

U.S. (former ratings): H–4, x x

Gleam. A clone of Lady Chamberlain g.

Goblin. g. and cl. AM 1939 ('Break of Day' × *griersonianum*). Despite the ratings, this is a pretty hardy plant and excellent for small gardens. Of neat habit, it grows to perhaps five feet, with sage-green leaves. The flowers are a vivid blend of rose and salmon, sometimes described as "rosy-orange". Their three-inch wide funnels are carried in a loose truss of seven and distinguished by the very large, irregularly lobed calyx, some lobes being more than an inch long. April–May,

The clone—

> **Goblin Pink** has pretty flowers of soft rose, with a golden throat.
>
> British ratings: C, ★
> Authors' dissent: B, ★ ★
> U.S.: H–4, 2/1

Golconda. g. ('Beau Brummell' × *dichroanthum*) 1939. Cross made 1932. A medium-sized and compact shrub with bright pink flowers. May–June.

Exbury ratings: B, ★

Goldfinger. A new clone of Parisienne g.

Golden Dream. A clone of Carita g.

Golden Horn. g. and cl. 1939, AM 1945. (*dichroanthum* × *elliottii*). A low, close-growing, compact plant of excellent quality, brilliantly coloured and quite hardy, with leaves near to sage-green with a brown indumentum beneath. The flowers are a vivid orange-red in the bud, opening to bells that are a blend of orange and deep salmon, with a brown mottling, and distinguished by a double calyx. They are borne in open, flat-topped trusses of about ten flowers in May. Its clone—

> **Persimmon** has the same useful habit, but is a rich, polished red, with minute, sooty powdering but without a double calyx.
>
> British ratings: B, ★ ★
> U.S.: H–4, 2/2

Golden Queen. A clone of Lady Chamberlain g.

Gondolier. g. ('Lady Harcourt' × *griersonianum*) 1947. Of average stature and loose habit, this plant flowers in trusses of large, bright red blossoms. May.

Exbury ratings: C, ★

Good Cheer. g. ('Lord Milner' × *sutchuenense*) 1939. A tall but well-clothed plant having white flowers with pink markings carried in a large, compact truss. April.

Exbury ratings: C, ★

Grace. g. (*fortunei* × *arboreum* forma *album*) 1939. A shrub with white flowers. *n.i.c.*

Grenada. g. ('Lady Rumbold' × *griersonianum*). Cross made 1932, introduced 1939. Of medium size and loose habit, having trusses of red flowers of average size. May.

Exbury ratings: C, ★

Grenadier. g. and cl. 1939, FCC 1943. ('Moser's Maroon' × *elliotti*). As befits its name, this is a tall and impressive rhododendron of well-knit, compact and sturdy bearing, upon which are generously displayed magnificent, globular trusses of large, blood-red flowers, each three and a half inches in diameter. A spectacular plant of superlative quality for the woodland glade. In Britain it does not normally exhibit a grenadier's toughness, needing protection from autumn frost, yet in the United States, where it is highly thought of, it has a higher hardiness rating. June.

British ratings: D, ★ ★ ★
U.S.: H–4, 3/2

Grenadine. g. and cl. 1939, AM 1956. ('Pauline' × *griersonianum*). A shrub of average size, good, compact habit and superior quality, bearing cerise flowers flushed deep orange in the throat with brown spots. A gay and showy plant for the woodland and sheltered places. This rhododendron was raised by Lionel de Rothschild but received its award when exhibited by Windsor in 1956. May–June.

Exbury ratings: C, ★ ★ ★

Grisette. g. (*arboreum* forma *album* × 'Dr Stocker') 1939. A tall but well-furnished plant that follows *arboreum* in both its growth habit and its flowers, which are of pure white with dark markings in the throat. April–May.

British ratings: B, ★ ★

Grosclaude. g. and cl. 1941, AM 1945. (*haematodes* × *eriogynum*). LR827 in the stud-book, introduced 1941. This very good cross between two red species of the finest quality brought forth a handsome offspring which is hardier than might be expected and fit to ornament the smaller garden as well as the larger. Of less than average height, it is neat and compact and the emergent young shoots are gaily clothed in a brown indumentum; as the leaves expand they turn dark green above but retain the indumentum below, where it changes to a dusky orange at maturity. On this background gleam quantities of open trusses of about ten or twelve ardent, blood-red, waxy bells, the petals of which are slightly waved at the edges. May.

British ratings: B, ★ ★ ★
U.S.: H–4, 3/3

Halcyone. g. (*souliei* × 'Lady Bessborough') 1940. A rhododendron of great floral beauty. The plant is of moderate and well-proportioned dimensions, well-furnished and ornamented with flowers of delicate but lively pink (not "cream" as in most reference books) which are wide open and cup-like and very gracefully carried in a lax, flat-topped truss. The influence of *R. souliei* is strong in both flower and foliage. Highly rated in the States. April–May.

British ratings: B, ★
Authors' dissent: B, ★★
U.S.: (to the grex) H–3, 3/3

There are now two clones—

Perdita. AM 1948. In the same style and build but the flowers are a lighter pink, fading to milk, with a few claret spots; a delightful plant.

Sandling. AM 1965. Rhodamine pink, flushed amber in the throat, recently exhibited by Major A. E. Hardy.

Happy. g. ('Pauline' × *griffithianum*) 1940. A moderately sized shrub of good habit with pink flowers marked with a deeper patch. May.

Exbury ratings: C, ★

Hawk. g. and cl. 1940, AM 1949. (*wardii* × 'Lady Bessborough'). In this now classic grex is included Rothschild's highest achievement in the search for pure yellow. It created a great stir when introduced by his son and set a new standard for woodland rhododendrons in this colour. Rothschild made the cross twice. It takes its name from HMS *Hawk*, the best known of the three styles which the Admiralty gave to Exbury House during the war. The stud-book entry (LR708) shows that the first cross was made on the *wardii* of Kingdon-Ward's 4170, which was the AM form as exhibited by Exbury.

The Hawks grow at Exbury about twelve feet high, in a rather loose and open fashion, sometimes rather drawn up by the trees, but always graceful. In 'Hawk' itself the flowers dispose themselves in an elegant and refined truss, airily borne without crowding. Apricot in the bud, they are sulphur-coloured and funnel-shaped, with deeply emarginate lobes. April–May.

British ratings for 'Hawk' AM: C, ★★
U.S.: (for the grex) H–4, 3/2

There are several clones—

Amour is a pure pale yellow.

Beaulieu Hawk is pale yellow.

Crest, FCC 1953. This is the supreme achievement in its field and undoubtedly the finest of the Hawk group. The large and immaculate truss is composed of about twelve flowers, beautifully poised and of great floral distinction. The apricot buds open primrose, which merges into a deeper hue around the throat on the upper segments. When 'Crest' was brought before the Rhododendron Committee of the RHS, some members doubted at first if it was really a 'Hawk'. It ensued from Lionel de Rothschild's second cross, when perhaps he used a different *R. wardii*. This might account for the different floral style, build and quality. In 'Crest' the blossoms are much larger and more open-mouthed ("shallow-campan-ulate") than in other Hawks and this makes the truss better furnished.

'Crest' first came into full bloom in the early 1950s and ever since then it has flowered profusely. The original FCC plant is now fourteen feet high. It is unaffected by frost or wind and seems to justify a hardiness rating of "B".

British ratings: C, ★ ★ ★ ★

U.S.: H–3, 4/2

Exbury Hawk. AM 1949. Clear yellow.

Hawk Kestrel is described as "rich" yellow.

British ratings: C, ★ ★

Hawk Merlin is another shade of yellow.

Jervis Bay AM 1951. Considered the best of the Hawks until the appearance of 'Crest' and still a distinguished rhododendron in its own right. Here the sulphur of the slightly frilled flower is distinctly stamped with a deep red eye, which is the imprint of its *wardii* parent.

British ratings: C, ★ ★ ★

U.S.: H–4, 3/2

Hereward. g. ('Dolly' × *griersonianum*) 1940. Rosy pink. *n.i.c.*

Herga. g. ('Break of Day' × 'Lady Bessborough') 1940. Pale yellow flowers with a dark stamp in the throat. May.

Exbury ratings: C, ★

Hermes. g. (*dichroanthum* ssp. *apodectum* × 'Lady Bessborough') 1940. A good plant of less than average size. Spreading, compact and well-furnished, this variety has showy, bell-shaped flowers of orange with pink markings, carried in loose trusses of becoming style. May.

British ratings: B, ★ ★

Hesperides. g. ('Ayah' × *griersonianum*) 1940. A tall and erect shrub, but of good compact behaviour, with rose-pink flowers in a good, full truss. June.

Exbury ratings: B, ★

Hypatia. g. ('Mrs R. S. Holford' × *kyawii*) 1940. A tall plant, rather loose-growing, with full trusses of bright red flowers. Useful for late flowering, but not hardy. June–July.

Exbury ratings: D, ★

Iago. g. ('Romany Chai' × 'Lady Bessborough') 1941. This plant has an upright bearing but only average height and flowers in trusses of medium size. The flowers are rosy-crimson with a large patch of darker spots. May.

Exbury ratings: B, ★

Ibex. g. and cl. AM 1948. (*griersonianum* × *pocophorum*). Introduced 1941. This is an attractive plant of less than average size and of trim, open habit. It bears trusses that are rather dome-shaped and composed of about ten rose-red flowers with darker spotting in the upper petals, white filaments and black anthers. The under surfaces of the narrow, sage-green leaves are densely felted with a brown indumentum. May–June.

British ratings: B, ★ ★

U.S.: H–5, 1/2

Ibis. g. ('Adelaide' × *griersonianum*) 1941. A fairly compact shrub of average size, with cerise flowers carried in a very good truss. April–May.

Exbury ratings: C, ★★

Icarus. g. AM 1947. ('A. Gilbert' × *dichroanthum* ssp. *herpesticum*). This is a beautiful rhododendron with parti-coloured flowers of a delightful blend. The shrub is of a little less than average dimensions, well-balanced and compact. The flowers, six or seven-lobed, carried in a flat-topped truss of eight, are a deep rose-pink in the bud, opening to biscuit-coloured bells, shaded rose, with perhaps an overall suggestion of orange. The pedicels are chestnut and glandular. May. There is a no less beautiful clone—

> **Organdie,** AM 1947, in which the leaves are a little smaller and the five-lobed flowers pale lemon-yellow with a margining of rose and a small pink zone at the base of the petals, carried on pale green pedicels.
>
> British ratings: B, ★★★

Icenia. g. ('Moser's Maroon' × 'Lady Bessborough') 1934, introduced 1941. Of average size and fairly loose habit, this variety carries pink flowers in a good, compact truss. May.

Exbury ratings: B, ★

Ida. g. ('J. G. Millais' × *neriiflorum*) 1934. Rose. *n.i.c.*

Idaho. g. ('Dolly' × *elliottii*) 1941. Of erect habit but average height, this flowers freely in well-knit trusses of brick-red. A good sort. May–June.

Exbury ratings: C, ★★

Idealist. g. and cl. 1941, AM 1945, (*wardii* × 'Naomi'). LR903 in the stud-book. One of the most beautiful rhododendrons ever raised. The shrub is of average height, and, like most *wardii* offspring, of good proportions and neat habit and is well-dressed with ample foliage. The short, broad leaves are a soft green. It flowers profusely and displays its innumerable and well-built trusses with a touch of boldness.

For this cross L. de R. no doubt used his greenish-yellow AM form of *wardii*, which was from seed of Kingdon-Ward's 4170. Coral-pink in the bud, borne on long, erect stalks and in calyces of tawny-purple, the flowers open very wide in the manner of *wardii*, revealing a blossom that is heavily flushed opaline pink, which quickly fades and is absorbed by an overall hue of a delightful pale greenish-yellow, cool, refreshing, glowing with light and accompanied by anthers of deep cream. The flowers are elegantly balanced in trusses, ten to twelve blossoms in each. An 'Idealist' in full bloom is an arresting and moving spectacle.

'Idealist' is fully hardy, being capable of standing temperatures down to nearly zero Fahrenheit and could well bear the "A" rating but for the fear that its superlative blossoms might be bleached. Its season is April–May.

British ratings: B, ★★★
Authors' dissent: B, ★★★★
U.S.: H–4, 3/2

The new clone—

> **Vienna** was named from a second cross made after the war and was a

seedling out of a batch sent to Knap Hill Nursery, who introduced it in 1962. The flowers are pale yellow and of good form and quality.

Iliad. g. and cl. AM 1949. ('Nereid' × *kyawii*). Cross made in 1941. A most attractive but tender plant of dwarf and compact habit, densely clothed in deep-green leaves and animated by loose clusters of vivid, blood-red flowers of waxy texture on villose pedicels. Very acceptable in sheltered gardens for its flowering in June.

Exbury ratings: D, ★ ★

Illyria. g. ('Romany Chal' × *kyawii*) 1941. Of tall and loose habit, having large, dark green leaves and a fairly compact truss of rich crimson flowers, individually large. June–July.

Exbury ratings: C, ★

Ilona. g. (*valentinianum* × *auritum*) 1941. Rather tender, but of great charm and liberality. Small trusses of pale gold are showered in great abundance on an average-size shrub of good, restrained habit. April–May.

Exbury ratings: C or D ★ ★

Fig. 12
Floral forms: tubular campanulate
(*R. meddianum*, AM).

Impi. g. and cl. AM 1945. ('Moser's Maroon' × *sanguineum* ssp. *didymum*). This shrub is of distinctive floral character and quite hardy. As might be expected from the parentage, the funnel flowers, two inches long, are of a very dark, dusky red, but have a satiny texture and in certain lights they gleam brilliantly. They are carried on longish foot-stalks, are slightly frilled at the edges and borne in small trusses on a moderate-sized shrub of compact build. June.

British ratings: B, ★ ★
U.S.: H–3, 1/1

Inamorata. g. and cl. 1941, AM 1950. (*wardii* × *discolor*). Of robust habit, this most handsome rhododendron combines the characteristics of both parents, including their stalwart bearing. *R. discolor* appears in the rosette arrangement of the leaves and *wardii* in the wide-mouthed bowls, which are of soft yellow with a small, spotted crimson flush in the throat and carried on purple foot-stalks. Altogether a handsome plant, richly attired. May–June.

British ratings: B, ★ ★ ★

Inchmery. g. ('The Don' × *eriogynum*) 1941. A tall, upright, loose plant with deep pink, waxy flowers. June.

Exbury ratings: C, ★

Indiana. g. (*dichroanthum* ssp. *scyphocalyx* × *kyawii*) 1941. A shrub in which the strong character of the magnificent male parent, with its deep, bright green foliage, is married with the arresting orange of the *dichroanthum* sub-species, which is here appropriately speckled with dark red. The flowers are carried in an open and well-composed truss and the shrub is of well-knit character, somewhat above average height. A valuable and distinctive shrub for fairly sheltered gardens in June.

British ratings: C, ★ ★ ★
U.S.: H–5, 3/2

Indomitable. g. (*souliei* × 'General Sir John du Cane') 1941. A good rhododendron, growing fairly tall but well compacted and providing a liberal display of distinguished flowers in the fashion of *souliei*. They are large, widely open in the mouth, white with a tender pink flush and are carried in a well-composed truss of average size with a fresh and graceful air which is very welcome in June. Merits a higher rating when well grown.

British ratings: B, ★ ★

Ingrid. g. ('Tally Ho' × *griffithianum*) 1934. Tall and of loose habit, with pink flowers, individually large, carried in an open truss. June.

Exbury ratings: C, ★

Intrepid. g. ('Beau Brummell' × *kyawii*) 1941. Tall and loose growing, with broad, green leaves and roseate flowers borne in a fairly compact truss. May–June.

Exbury ratings: C, ★

Iola. g. (*valentinianum* × *edgeworthii*) 1941. Beautiful when in full flower, but rather tender, this makes a small, compact, well-ordered shrub decorated with bouquets of small blossoms of pale primrose. April.

Exbury ratings: D, ★

Iolanthe. g. ('Blanc-mange' × *kyawii*) 1941. Rather tender, this is another plant produced by L. de R. to prolong the season. Following *kyawii*, the plant is tall but fairly compact and its large, cerise flowers are borne in heavy trusses. July.

Exbury ratings: D, ★

Ironside. g. ('Midsummer' × *kyawii*) 1941. Another late one. Tall but well-furnished, it carries good trusses of large individual flowers in bright crimson. July.

Exbury ratings: C, ★

Isis. g. ('Carex' × *laxiflorum*) 1941. A not very successful white. *n.i.c.*

Islay. g. (*agapetum* × 'Romany Chai') 1941. Rich, bright scarlet. *n.i.c.*

Isme. g. (*wardii* × *venator*) 1941. A plant that is very attractive when in full flower, having small trusses of yellow flowers with rose markings on a shrub of moderate size and good habit. April–May.

Exbury ratings: C, ★

Ispahan. g. ('Fabia' × *wardii*) 1941. For small gardens with the right conditions this is a good shrub of low and spreading habit with showy flowers varying from tangerine to yellow, with a waxy polish, borne in a fairly loose and open truss in May.

Exbury ratings: C, ★

Istanbul. g. ('Mrs H. Stocker' × *elliottii*) 1941. A tall and fairly compact shrub bearing full trusses of red flowers in June.

Exbury ratings: C, ★

Istar. g. (*dichroanthum* × 'Naomi') 1941. Though not of the distinction one might have expected from its parentage, this is another good shrub for small gardens, having a low, spreading, compact habit. The flowers are yellow with pink markings, arranged in a fairly loose truss. Quite hardy. May.

Exbury ratings: B, ★

Ithica. g. (*dichroanthum* ssp. *scyphocalyx* × ssp. *septentrionale* × *eriogynum*) 1941. *n.i.c.*

Ivan. g. ('B. de Bruin' × *kyawii*) 1941. With the influence of *kyawii* strong, this is a tall, erect plant, with large, deep green leaves, needing protection from cold winds. The flowers are large, of a bright, clear crimson and carried in a good truss. July.

Exbury ratings: D, ★

Ivanhoe. g. and cl. 1941, AM 1945. ('Chanticleer' × *griersonianum*). A tall plant of rather loose habit, bearing good trusses of brilliant, red flowers, very faintly spattered with a deeper red on the upper petals. April–May.

Exbury ratings: C, ★ ★
U.S.: H–4, 2/2

Iviza. g. ('Fabia' × 'Bustard') 1941. An unusual rhododendron this. Of neat habit, the shrub grows not more than five feet high, with glossy, spoon-shaped leaves. The flowers, marked by a small double calyx, are pink and yellow in the bud, opening to long, glossy tubes of orange-salmon and borne in a rather lax truss. May–June. The clone—

Philomene has the same habit but the flowers are an attractive straw colour, tinted pink with green markings and a darker patch in the throat.

Exbury ratings: B, ★ ★

U.S. (former rating): H–4, x

Ivy. A clone of Lady Chamberlain g.

Jacobean. g. ('Bibiani' × *sanguineum* ssp. *haemaleum*) 1942. An average-sized shrub of good habit, bearing fairly compact trusses of distinctive, deep maroon flowers of medium size. April–May.

Exbury ratings: C, ★

Jacqueline. g. (*facetum* × 'Albatross') 1942. Late in flowering and of tall, compact build, this plant has flesh-pink flowers which are individually large and carried in a well-proportioned truss. June.

Exbury ratings: C, ★

Jacques. g. and cl. (*dichroanthum* × 'Day Dream') 1942. Of moderate size and normal habit, with flowers that are a blend of pink and orange. April–May.

Exbury ratings: C, ★

Jaipur. g. (*forrestii* var. *repens* × *meddianum*) 1942. This cross resulted in a very attractive, but rather tender, dwarf rhododendron which looks very handsome in sheltered rock gardens. Spreading generously in the manner of Forrest's celebrated dwarf and clothed in dark green, rounded leaves, it is decorated with large, drooping, deep crimson flowers which are evidence of a happy marriage. April–May.

Exbury ratings: D, ★ ★

U.S.: H–4, 3/1

Jalisco. g. and cl. ('Lady Bessborough' × 'Dido') 1942. LR833 in the Exbury stud-book. One of the most successful of Lionel de Rothschild's crossings in pursuit of his yellow ideal, this group includes some clones of very high merit. Some young plants resulting from this cross were among many that King George VI accepted from him. Registered in the year of L. de R.'s death during the war, 'Jalisco' did not come into prominence till after the war was over, when several fine clones were exhibited by Windsor, where they had enjoyed Sir Eric Savill's skilled attention.

'Jalisco' is a plant of average size and good behaviour, compact when not given too much tree cover, with broad, richly green leaves, five to six inches long, and bearing large, open trusses of delightful, waxy, maize-coloured florets, widely funnel-campanulate, beginning to bloom at the end of May and continuing well into June. The clones are—

Exbury Jalisco. Of a dusky yellow with a faint green undertone, this is considered by many to be on a par with 'Jalisco Goshawk'.

Exbury ratings: B, ★ ★ ★

Jalisco Eclipse. AM 1948. Primrose, with dark crimson eye and speckling in the throat and streaked externally with crimson. The narrow, elliptic leaf is distinctive.

British ratings: B, ★ ★

Jalisco Elect. AM 1948. Primrose with paler lobes, some chestnut spots and a petaloid calyx. Up to ten flowers in a rather loose truss.

British ratings: B, ★ ★

Jalisco Emblem, 1948. Pale yellow with a dark patch.

Jalisco Goshawk, FCC 1954. The star of this group, which created a great impression when shown by Windsor in the last year of the war, but of course did not become widely known until afterwards. Its beautiful flowers are a shade of "mimosa" with some crimson stippling.

British ratings: B, ★ ★ ★

Jalisco Janet, 1948. Yellow.

Jalisco Jubilant. AM 1966. A delightful new clone exhibited by Exbury. The widely campanulate flowers, airily poised in a truss of up to fourteen florets and seated within a yellow calyx nearly an inch long, are flushed with poppy-red in the bud, opening buttercup-yellow, deepening in the throat, which is faintly marked with green spots.

Lindberg, 1954. Yellow.

Jamaica. g. ('Break of Day' × *eriogynum*) 1942. A low and widely spreading plant of loose build, bearing good trusses of deep orange flowers. April–May.

Exbury ratings: C, ★ ★

Janet. g. and cl. 1942, AM 1950. ('Avalanche' × 'Dr Stocker'). This is a very fine and distinguished rhododendron indeed, one of the many from Exbury that have not yet been widely distributed. It develops into a tall, stately, most impressive plant, very well clothed and of fine bearing. It is large in all its parts. The very big trusses are boldly displayed and are composed of very large and beautiful flowers that measure five inches at the mouth of the trumpets. They are white with a deep crimson stain at the base within.

'Janet' is a very handsome plant for a large and sheltered situation, typical of a late April rhododendron and in the very highest rank among the big hybrids.

Exbury ratings: C, ★ ★ ★ ★

Jan Steen. g. and cl. ('Fabia' × 'Lady Bessborough') Preliminary Commendation 1950. A fairly tall and erect shrub inclined to branch loosely, but attractive and showy when in full bloom. The wide-mouthed flowers are in azalea-like tones of orange and yellow and are carried in loose trusses, erectly held in late May.

British ratings: B, ★

Jason. g. (*lacteum* × 'Penjerrick') 1942, AM 1966. A fine plant which has had to wait a long time for recognition, though always well thought of at Exbury. The campanulate flowers are pinkish in the bud, opening to pale ivory with a primrose flush on the upper petals, a distinct pink tint in the veination and small, very deep pink markings in the throat. (The RHS citation says colour between chartreuse green and primrose yellow, shaded at base to ivory). They are carried in a tall truss of fifteen to seventeen florets. The plant stands fifteen to eighteen feet high, with an upright, rather loose carriage and sturdy, deep green broadly elliptic foliage seven and a half inches long. The habit and general appearance show the *lacteum* influence strongly. April.

Exbury ratings: C, ★ ★ ★

Jasper. g. and cl. (*dichroanthum* × 'Lady Bessborough') 1942. A low and spreading shrub bearing loose trusses of pale orange flowers in May. Quite hardy. The clone—

> **Jasper Pimento,** has the same build, but the flowers are deep orange-red.
>
> British ratings: B, ★
>
> U.S.: H–3, 1/2

Jerez. A clone of Fred Wynniatt g.

Jeritsa. g. and cl. AM 1951. (introduced 1942) (*griffithianum* × 'Lady Bessborough'). Another wartime introduction that had to wait several years for recognition. This is a tall, well-built, leafy shrub, with attractive foliage of a mat olive-green, from which spring abundant quantities of large, heavy trusses of pale "mimosa" yellow, enlivened by a small crimson zone and specklings within. A reliable and very decorative plant, flowering in May.

Exbury ratings: B, ★ ★ ★

Jervis Bay. A clone of Hawk g.

Jester. g. (*dichroanthum* × 'Naomi'). Rather late-flowering, of low and spreading build and bearing loose trusses of lively flowers in yellow with pink markings. May–June.

Exbury ratings: B, ★ ★

Jibuti. g. and cl. 1942, AM 1949 (*griersonianum* × 'Gill's Triumph'). Tall and erect, this plant bears, with the greatest freedom, large, conical trusses of campanulate flowers in a shade of deep rose on viscous pedicels in June.

Exbury ratings: B, ★ ★

Jiusepa. g. (*dichroanthum* × 'Day Dream') 1942. Of average size and of good compact build. The flowers are a blend of biscuit and yellow and are borne in a loose truss of average size in May.

Exbury ratings: C, ★

Joana. g. (*wardii* × 'Albatross') 1942. White and cream. *n.i.c.*

Joanita. g. and cl. (*lacteum* × *caloxanthum*) 1942. A wartime introduction of no little merit, not widely known. It became in time a big shrub of 18 feet, with broad leaves, near to the male parent, and of a well-knit build. The parentage virtually guarantees yellow flowers, and these are of a shining green-gold tincture, with a deeper golden style, in handsome bells enlivened with a typical *lacteum* eye in crimson. They are arranged in an open and graceful truss. It is reported, like some other *lacteum* hybrids, to be sometimes "difficult", but when established it is an attractive rhododendron that gleams brightly in the woodland, where it begins to shine at the end of April. See 'Costa del Sol', p. 112.

Exbury ratings: C, ★ ★ ★

Jocelyne. g. and cl. 1942, FCC 1956, AM 1954. (*lacteum* × *calophytum*). An introduction that has only recently come to the front and one of the new glories of Exbury at the season when, in Mrs Lionel's words, it "wears its Riviera dress". The plant is tall, of handsome bearing and well proportioned. It is clothed with leaves that are mat green above and lightly coated with an indumentum beneath. From this well-built structure emerge large trusses of superlative quality, up to twenty-two blossoms to a truss. They are in mother-of-pearl tones, lit up with a crimson mark in the throat, typical of *lacteum* offspring, the whole flower gleaming with light. Altogether a superb rhododendron for woodland or mild coastal gardens. March–April.   Exbury ratings: C, ★ ★ ★ ★

Jordan. g. (*dichroanthum* × *griffithianum*) 1942. A good shrub of average size and well-behaved growth, bearing fairly loose trusses of pale orange with a trace of pink. Very colourful and attractive when in full bloom in April.

British ratings: C, ★ ★

Josephine. g. (*wardii* × 'Ayah'). Crossed 1925, introduced 1942. Tall and upright but of closely knit habit, this good shrub is clothed in glossy, deep green foliage and has well-composed trusses of deep cream or wan yellow. May.

Exbury ratings: B, ★ ★

Joyance. g. (*wardii* × *dichroanthum* ssp. *scyphocalyx*) 1942. A shrub somewhat below average height, of good habit, producing small trusses of cream sprinkled with salmon or pale orange markings. May.

Exbury ratings: C, ★

Joyful. A clone of Fred Wynniatt g.

Judith. g. (Loderi g. × 'Gen. Sir John du Cane') 1942. White with a pink flush. *n.i.c.*

Jungfrau. cl. AM May 1966 ('Marie Antoinette' × ?). Here one of L. de R.'s less distinguished hybrids has been crossed with an unidentified mate to produce an offspring of considerable merit. The shrub is tall and well built with dark green foliage of medium length, bearing huge, conical trusses of some twenty pale pink, openly campanulate florets. May.

Exbury ratings: B, ★ ★ ★

Jutland. g. and cl. 1942, AM 1947. (*elliottii* × 'Bellerophon'). This is a most desirable, late-flowering but rather tender shrub of average size and compact build. It has bold foliage of a soft, rich green, six and a half inches long, with recurved margins, and is dressed with handsome, high-domed trusses composed of up to twenty bells of fine floral quality. They are coloured geranium-lake, shining with the incandescent glitter of *elliottii*, flecked with darker red marks, and are distinguished by five conspicuous nectar pouches. The U.S. ratings are to be noted. June.

Exbury ratings: D, ★ ★ ★
U.S.: H–4, 3/3

Karkov. g. and cl. 1943, AM 1947. (*griersonianum* × 'Red Admiral'). Of normal size and habit, this is florally quite a distinctive rhododendron. It bears well-composed, globular trusses of about sixteen funnel-shaped flowers, which are a carmine-rose, evenly but faintly spotted, the margins of which are slightly waved. The leaves are narrowly elliptic, six inches long. April–May.

British ratings: C, ★ ★
U.S.: H–5, 1/2

Kiev. g. and cl. 1943, AM 1950. (*elliottii* × 'Barclayi Robert Fox'). Here we have a fairly new rhododendron of remarkable floral splendour and quality, but, as might be guessed from the parentage, of a low hardiness rating. 'Kiev' is the darkest red in the Exbury Gardens, its depth of colour emphasized by the almost sooty spotting on the three upper lobes, derived from *elliottii*, against which the white anthers sparkle like tiny stars. In some lights the flowers, which have a brilliant, waxy polish, appear almost black, but when the sun is shining through them they are a glowing, luminous blood-red. They are impressively arranged in a flat-topped truss of twelve. The shrub tends towards the tall, vigorous, lank growth which is effective only in woodland and it is one of Edmund de Rothschild's favourites. April–May.

Exbury ratings: D, ★ ★ ★ ★
U.S.: H–4, 3/2

Kilimanjaro. g. and cl. 1943, FCC 1947. (*elliottii* × 'Dusky Maid'). Another superlative rhododendron of low hardiness rating. The shrub is of average height and good, close-growing habit. Its large flowers, "burning with celestial light" kindled by the spark of *elliottii*, are of an intensely rich and luminous red, similar to the colour of red currants, and they are arrayed in a large, round, dramatic truss of some eighteen blossoms. A sumptuous, exciting and really outstanding hybrid, not flowering until June.

In some seasons at Exbury 'Kilimanjaro' builds up a truss of tremendous proportions, with the largest flowers of all the reds, but always perfectly formed. 'Moser's Maroon' is again in the sap, through the male parent.

Exbury ratings: C, or D, ★ ★ ★ ★

Kingcup. g. and cl. AM 1943 (*dichroanthum* × 'Bustard'). A low-growing shrub of compact habit with yellow, tubular flowers of a gleaming, waxen texture, arranged in loose trusses that are rather flat-topped. May.

Exbury ratings: C, ★ ★
U.S.: H–3, 2/2

Kingsway. cl. (*discolor* × *zeylanicum*). A new, late-flowering plant that received a Preliminary Commendation in 1960. It grows into a big but compact plant and bears white flowers that are flushed with pink, with still deeper pink in the throat, arranged on a large truss of good form. June.

Exbury ratings: C, ★ ★

Kola. g. ('Isabella' × 'Tally Ho'). Crossed in 1938, introduced 1947. Pink flowers on a well-shaped truss are borne on a tall plant of rather loose habit in June.

Exbury ratings: C, ★

Lady Berry. g. and cl. 1935, FCC 1949; AM 1937. ('Rosy Bell' × 'Royal Flush'). A magnificent but tender rhododendron, of the highest ornamental value in favourable conditions. In general style it resembles the more famous 'Lady Chamberlain' and 'Lady Rosebery', but is less hardy and so less familiar.

The shrub is of moderate size and erect bearing, clothed in polished, aromatic, sea-green foliage, which is densely scaly beneath. The truss is loose and open and is made up of five pendulous flowers, like long, slim trumpets, which are of fleshy texture and about three inches long, five-lobed. Their colouring is delightful, being rosy-opal within and red without, paling gradually towards the mouth.

In western maritime counties 'Lady Berry' is an outstanding example of the *cinnabarinum* floral style. April–May.

British ratings: D, ★ ★ ★ ★
U.S.: H–5, 3/3

Lady Bessborough. g. and cl. FCC 1933. (*discolor* × *campylocarpum* var. *elatum*). LR100 in the stud book. One of the most famous of the Rothschild rhododendrons and one of the earliest fruits of L. de R.'s hybridizing. In consequence, it has been used for further matings and is a parent of many of Exbury's finest rhodos, including 'Hawk', 'Jalisco', 'Day Dream', and 'Halcyone'—a very fine record for any parent.

Named after one of Mrs Lionel de Rothschild's life-long friends, 'Lady Bessborough' is a big, upstanding shrub of open habit, with foliage of *discolor* persuasion, hardy to below zero F. and flowering profusely at the end of May and into June, when it is a wonderful spectacle. The flowers are wide open funnels, prettily fringed and slightly scented. Apricot in the bud, they open in a tone of deep, rich cream, rather like Cotswold stone, are marked in the throat with a dark red eye and are carried in a large, loose truss.

The clones in the group, of which the second and fourth signalize Lord Bessborough's term as Governor-General of Canada, are—

Belle, a very pale lemon.

Montreal, pink in the bud opening to the typical deep cream or biscuit.

Old Olson (or 'Ole Olson'), an American clone.

Ottawa, a blend of orange-pink, turning white.

Roberte, FCC 1936. The Christian name of Lady Bessborough herself. A particularly beautiful clone, with flowers of rose-pink, speckled with red.

British ratings: B, ★ ★ ★ ★
U.S.: (for the grex) H–3, 3/2

Ladybird. g. and cl. AM 1933. (*discolor* × 'Corona'). This is a fine, vigorous hybrid that grows to great size, with a rather open habit, clothed with shapely leaves of a glossy green. It is richly dressed with enormous trusses of large, widely expanded flowers of a lovely, deep coral-pink with a deeper eye. It flowers profusely and is a good example of a hybrid inheriting the best qualities of both parents. May–June.

British ratings: B, ★ ★ ★
U.S.: H–3, 2/2

Lady Chamberlain. g. and cl. 1930, FCC 1931. (*cinnabarinum* var. *roylei* × 'Royal Flush' orange form). Even more famous than 'Lady Bessborough', but not nearly as hardy. 'Lady Chamberlain' and her brood are something different from the general run of rhododendrons, being characterized by the pendulous, flared

Fig. 13
Floral forms: tubular
(*R*. 'Lady Chamberlain', FCC).

tubes of *R. cinnabarinum* (which is in the male parent's sap also), but much larger than in the species.

The result is a truss of very distinctive and highly ornamental character, having five or more of these slim and elegant trumpets, loosely arrayed. The colour varies from orange to salmon, suffused with rose and shining in the sun with the luminosity of *cinnabarinum*. It flowers with prodigal abandon.

The shrub is of medium size and erect bearing, with beautiful leaves, the young growths tinted with blue before turning sea-green. It flowers in April–May and is highly esteemed in America. It is LR178 in the stud-book, with 'Lady Rosebery' immediately following.

British ratings: C, ★ ★ ★ ★
U.S.: (to the grex) H–5, 3/3

88

The following are the clones—

Apricot Lady Chamberlain, has flowers of that colour.

U.S. ratings: H–4, 3/3

Bodnant Yellow is orange-buff (introduced by Lord Aberconway).

Chelsea is orange and pink.

British ratings: C, ★ ★

Exbury Lady Chamberlain, FCC 1931, is orange or yellow, overlaid with salmon.

British ratings: C, ★ ★ ★ ★

Gleam is orange with petals tipped crimson.

British ratings: C, ★★

U.S.: H–5, 3/3

Golden Queen, FCC 1947, is a soft yellow, shaded orange.

British ratings: C, ★ ★

Ivy is a tone of salmon.

Lady Chamberlain Seville is marmalade colour.

U.S. ratings: H–5, 3/3

Oriflamme is orange-red.

British ratings: C, ★ ★

Salmon Trout is salmon-pink.

British ratings: C, ★ ★ ★

The reputed clone 'Lady Chamberlain Etna' is not known at Exbury, but see under Lady Rosebery g.

Lady Montagu. g. and cl. AM 1931 (*griffithianum* × *thomsonii*). Of tall and loose habit, with loose trusses of fairly large flowers that are pink within and nearly red, a darker flush on the exterior. May.

Exbury ratings: C, ★

Lady Rosebery. g. and cl. 1930, FCC 1932. (*cinnabarinum* var. *roylei* × 'Royal Flush' pink form). Another of the most famous of L. de R.'s early raisings, equalling 'Lady Chamberlain' in reputation and having a close floral similarity, but having pink predominating as the result of using a different colour form of J. C. Williams's 'Royal Flush'. The plant has the same habit as 'Lady Chamberlain' and the tubes or slender trumpets are crimson on the outside and a bright, rose-red within, sparkling with the fire of rubies. Another very high-ranking variety in the United States in districts where the climate suits it. It is LR179 in the stud-book, immediately following the mating that resulted in 'Lady Chamberlain'. April–May.

Technically, 'Lady Rosebery' should be regarded as a clone of Lady Chamberlain g., since they are the same cross, despite the colour variations of 'Royal Flush'.

British ratings: C, ★ ★ ★ ★

U.S.: (to the grex) H–5, 4/3

The clones of this group are:

Lady Rosebery Dalmeny. Soft saline pink.

Lady Rosebery Etna. Rose.

British ratings: C, ★ ★ ★ ★

Lady Rosebery Pink Dawn. A clone registered by the late Lord Digby.
Lady Rosebery Pink Delight.

British ratings: C, ★ ★ ★ ★

Lanyon. A clone of Marshall g.

Leo. g. and cl. 1947, AM 1948. ('Britannia' × *elliottii*). Named after one of L. de R.'s sons, and not to be confused with the azalea of the same name, this is a magnificent rhododendron that has not yet been widely distributed. The parent *elliottii* gives it a slight tenderness, but in suitable climates it is a shrub of dazzling brilliance, flowering in great profusion. The campanulate flowers, embellished with pink filaments and brown anthers, are a fervent crimson-scarlet, aflame in a huge, round truss of up to twenty-five. The shrub is of average size and excellent habit and is furnished with very dark green leaves. A wonderful plant in woodland, enjoying a high status in America though not officially rated in Britain. May–June.

Exbury ratings: C, ★ ★ ★ ★
U.S.: H–3, 4/3

Leonore. g. and cl. 1947, AM 1948 (*auriculatum* × *kyawii*). One of the very late sorts that L. de R. raised to prolong the season, surprising the visitor as he walks through the woods in July, or even in August. It grows into a huge plant of good habit, but is not hardy. Its slightly hairy leaves are a bright green, arranged in rosettes, coated beneath with a brownish down, and its tall, loose trusses are composed of about a dozen large flowers in red flushed with carmine.

Exbury ratings: D, ★ ★

Lindberg, a clone of Jalisco g.

Lionel's Triumph. g. and cl. AM 1954. (*lacteum* × 'Naomi'). An outstanding variety of recent introduction considered by Exbury to be of the highest rating, but not yet widely distributed. It is one of the "hidden treasures" left behind by L. de R. No doubt *R. lacteum* had been exerting its retarding influence. As related in Part II, it was discovered at the back of the estate yard, overgrown, and unnoticed after the neglect of the war years, until it first bloomed in 1954. It won its award immediately, but it was not until it was planted out in an ampler environment that its full splendour was exhibited.

'Lionel's Triumph' expresses in its name the quality that Exbury ascribes to this discovery. It grows into a big plant of commanding bearing with good foliage and the years have shown it to be quite hardy. The flowers are borne in magnificent trusses of up to eighteen florets, themselves individually large. They are rose-pink in the bud, opening to a deep, rich, Cornish cream colour, flushed opaline pink on the margins, with little crimson flashes sparkling in the throat. The pink margins wane as the flower expands. April–May.

Exbury ratings: B, ★ ★ ★ ★

Major. g. (*haematodes* × *thomsonii*) 1947. A rather low and fairly compact shrub with open trusses of polished, crimson-scarlet flowers, yellow style, white filaments and the *thomsonii* calyx; a little shy in some years, but very showy when in full bloom. April–May.

Charles Michael is a clone exhibited by Mr C. Williams in 1948.

British ratings: B, ★

Mandalay. g. (*haematodes* × *venator*) 1947. The deep red flowers in a loose truss make a very showy plant, which grows to little more than four feet, nicely compacted. April–May.

Exbury ratings: C, ★
U.S.: H–4, 2/2

Marathon. g. ('Pauline' × *elliottii*) 1947. A somewhat tender shrub of moderate height and spreading habit, bearing bright red flowers in a truss of normal size. June.

Exbury ratings: C, or D, ★

Marie Antoinette. g. ('Albatross' × 'Ariel') 1945. White flowers, flushed with pink and flecked with green markings, are borne in a well-formed truss on a tall and upright plant. May–June.

Exbury ratings: B, ★

Mariloo. g. and cl. ('Dr Stocker' × *lacteum*) 1941. Named after Mrs Lionel de Rothschild and a rhododendron of the very front rank. Though *lacteum* hybrids are often difficult and slow, 'Mariloo' is an exception. It grows well and fairly fast and Hanger in his day described it as "the best of all the R. *lacteum* hybrids at Exbury", adding that "the extra large and perfect trusses outshine most rhododendrons I know for quality and size."

'Mariloo' grows in the tall, expansive manner typical of Exbury, clothed with the bold foliage of *lacteum*, and bears lemon-yellow flowers, flushed with green, of great beauty and charm in a big truss, well packed. The florets are first tubular-campanulate, but the mouth later becomes fully expanded, when the green tint begins to recede.

The shrub is not of the first hardiness, its young leaves being sensitive to cold winds, but otherwise it is a superlative plant that gleams almost luminously in the woodland in April.

British ratings: C, ★ ★ ★ ★
U.S.: (to the grex) H–4, 4/2

There are two very fine clones to note:

Mariloo Eugenie, AM 1950, bears magnificent and heavy trusses loaded with up to seventeen blossoms, which are of pale cream with a crimson flash and small crimson spots at the base of the throat.

British ratings: C, ★ ★ ★ ★

Mariloo Gilbury, AM 1943. Of superb floral quality, being of a pale, creamy pink with deep pink stripes on the back of each segment of the bloom.

British ratings: C, ★ ★ ★ ★

Marshall. g. and cl. (*haematodes* × *elliottii*) 1947. This is a reliable shrub of little height, but of spreading habit, well-furnished with deep green leaves that have a slight fawn indumentum. The flowers are bright scarlet arranged in a medium-sized truss. May.

Lanyon, a clone of this grex, was exhibited by Colonel E. Bolitho.

British ratings: C, ★

Mary Roxburghe. A clone of Sir Frederick Moore g.

Melody. g. ('Loderi Venus' × 'General Sir John de Cane') 1950. A tall, well-furnished plant with creamy-pink flowers in a good, well-packed and shapely truss. May–June.

Exbury ratings: B, ★

Melrose. g. (*dichroanthum* × 'Avocet'). Crossed 1930, introduced 1947. Pale pink. Not of high merit.

Memory. A clone of Gipsy King g.

Michele. g. (*griersonianum* × 'Afghan') 1947. Red flowers in a good and shapely truss are borne on a plant of moderate size and loose growth. April–May.

Exbury ratings: C, ★

Minerva. g. ('Sir Frederick Moore' × *elliottii*). Crossed 1939, introduced 1947. Pink flowers in a good and large truss on a tall plant. June.

Exbury ratings: C, ★

Minnehaha. g. ('Corona' × *souliei*) 1947. A showy little rhodo with pink, waxy flowers gleaming in a small, loose truss on a low and spreading plant. April–May.

Exbury ratings: C, ★

Mohamet. g. and cl. AM 1945. (*dichroanthum* × 'Tally Ho'). A rather tender plant, but stands fairly low temperatures in the United States. The leaves are pale green with a light fawn indumentum beneath on a shrub of moderate growth and open habit. The flowers are bright scarlet, individually large, frilled at the margins, with large, petaloid calyces of the same colour, and are borne in a loose truss of five or six blooms. May.

Exbury ratings: D, ★ ★
U.S.: H–5, 2/2

Montreal. A clone of Lady Bessborough g.

Moonbeam. g. ('Naomi' × *griffithianum*) 1947. Very pale primrose flowers in a nicely formed truss on a tall plant in May. Not to be confused with the azalea of the same name.

Exbury ratings: C, ★

Moonglow. g. ('Loderi Venus' × 'Lady Bessborough') 1946. Pale pink flowers in a truss of good form carried on a tall plant. May.

Exbury ratings: B, ★
U.S.: H–3, 2/1

Mosaique. g. and cl. AM 1945. (*ambiguum* × 'Cinnkeys'). This is a small and very close-knit shrub with small, narrow-lobed flowers of wan yellow, flushed bright red at the base, not expanding fully, carried in a truss of about twelve flowers. May–June.

Exbury ratings: C, ★

Mouton Rothschild. cl. AM 1958. ('Beau Brummell' × *elliottii*). A rhododendron that flowers with the utmost profusion and brilliance of colour, but not of the highest degree of hardiness, having *R. eriogynum* in the sap on the female side, as well as *R. elliottii*. The plant is of moderate growth and loose habit and is dressed with handsome trusses of conical outline well packed with gleaming, bright red bells of waxy texture. June.

Exbury ratings: C, ★ ★ ★

Mrs. Leopold de Rothschild. g. and cl. AM 1933. ('B. de Bruin' × *griersonianum*). Another very free-flowering rhododendron. Of moderate size, it is of close-growing form. Its abundant, light red, widely expanded flowers are sprinkled with fawn spots and are carried in a good, shapely truss. April–May.

Exbury ratings: C, ★ ★

U.S.: H–3, 2/2

Nancy. g. ('Prometheus' × *neriiflorum*) 1931. Pink. *n.i.c.*

Naomi. g. and cl. 1926, AM 1933. ('Aurora' × *fortunei*) LR108 in the stud-book. One of the world's premier hybrids. 'Naomi' has claim to being the finest grex that L. de R. ever raised and it was certainly his favourite. Named after his youngest daughter, it has almost everything that a rhododendron should have—splendid, sturdy, well-filled growth, with flowers of the utmost charm, a honeyed breath and produced with the most opulent generosity. It is completely hardy, rated in the United States to withstand temperatures far below those encountered in Britain. Although given a "B" rating in Britain, some of Exbury's plants are grown in full sun. Certain of the clones have the highest possible ratings in one country or the other, or in both.

The original plants are some fifteen to eighteen feet high and twelve to fifteen feet wide and all are smothered in blossom right down to ground level every year. At the end of April and in May they are a magnificent and moving spectacle, the magnet of the thousands of people who visit Exbury for the "open days" at that time.

The flowers of Naomi's family, which are large, wide-mouthed and lily-like, all have an opaline or mother-of-pearl quality in their tinctures, which are in tones of tender pinks and yellows. In 'Naomi' itself the colour is a delicate pink, distinctly undertoned with yellow—a charming combination made the more so by its sweet scent. The influence of *R. fortunei* (which is also in the ancestry of L. de R.'s own 'Aurora') is strongly evident in the scent, the hardiness, the good foliage and the lilac-pink that tinctures several of the clones, while the pink of 'Aurora' dominates others. We may also trace *R. griffithianum*, another ancestor of 'Aurora', likewise carrying scent.

L. de R. subsequently used 'Naomi' freely for further matings and among her particularly distinguished children are to be numbered 'Lionel's Triumph', 'Carita' and 'Idealist'—a record of which any parent might be proud.

British ratings: B, ★ ★ ★

Authors' dissent: A, ★ ★ ★

Former U.S. rating for the grex: H–2, x x x

The 'Naomi' clones to note are as follows, but see also 'Paris', p. 113.

Exbury Naomi. Perhaps the pearl of them all and L. de R.'s own favourite. The flowers, deep cerise in the bud, open to biscuit, tinged with lilac-pink, with engaging green filaments and style.

British ratings: B, ★ ★ ★ ★
U.S.: −, 4/4

Naomi Astarte, pink, shaded yellow and with a yellow throat.

British ratings: B, ★ ★
U.S.: H−4, 4/4

Naomi Carissima, pale pink flushed with cream.

U.S. ratings: H−3, 2/3

Naomi Early Dawn, pale pink.

U.S. ratings: H−3, 3/3

Naomi Glow, deep pink, deepening further in the throat.

U.S. ratings: H−3, 4/4

Naomi Hope, pink, tinted with mauve.

U.S. ratings: H−3, 4/3

Naomi Nautilus, AM 1938, rose, flushed pale orange. Flowers very large, frilled, flattening out.

British ratings: B, ★ ★ ★
U.S.: H−2, 4/4

Naomi Nereid, deep crimson and lavender.

British ratings: B, ★ ★ ★
U.S.: H−3, 3/4

Naomi Pink Beauty, uniform, satiny pink.

British ratings: B, ★ ★ ★
U.S.: H−3, 3/4

Naomi Pixie, deep pink, red centred. *n.i.c.* at Exbury.

U.S. ratings: H−3, 4/4

Naomi Stella Maris, FCC 1939, buff, shaded lilac-pink, the flowers larger, the trusses fuller, the leaves longer than in other clones.

British ratings: B, ★ ★ ★ ★
U.S.: H−3, 4/4

Nehru. g. (*griersonianum* × 'Huntsman') 1946. Scarlet flowers in a showy truss of good form on a tall, upright plant of loose habit. April–May.

Exbury ratings: C, ★

Nicholas. cl., AM 1965 (*ponticum* × ?). This entirely new rhododendron, named after Edmund de Rothschild's eldest son, is a great surprise and an exciting one. In an establishment where everything is carefully regulated and recorded, it is one of only three rhododendrons of which the parentage is unknown. Conceivably the bee was responsible. The one thing certain is that R. *ponticum* was one of the parents, for the polished, dark green, pointed leaves are very clearly of that species.

The colour is most unusual—a bright, glowing purple, known as "petunia purple" in the Horticultural Colour Chart, diversified in the throat and the upper lobe with a large and spreading white patch, on which appear a number of small, green spots. The flowers are in the form of wide-mouthed funnels, and are carried in a large, shapely, closely packed truss of about nineteen blooms and are produced in the greatest abundance. They are of fine quality and bear little or no resemblance to those of *R. ponticum*.

'Nicholas' is one of three similar shrubs at Exbury that have attained proportions of about twelve by twelve feet. The other two are inferior in colour but 'Nicholas' is far too good to be denied increase, especially as it fills a very patent blank in the colour range of the larger rhodos. Moreover, it is completely hardy and should be quite at home wherever rhododendrons will grow. At Exbury it grows in full exposure. The season is May–June.

Exbury ratings: A, ★ ★ ★

Nimrod. g. and cl. (*irroratum* 'Polka Dot' × *calophytum*) 1963. This is a new introduction of high quality and great floral charm. The parentage is strongly marked, first of all in the tall, strong, well-built bearing of the shrub, which one might expect from both. *R. calophytum* shows itself in the long broad leaves, and 'Polka Dot' (Exbury's own award form of *R. irroratum*) in the tubular-campanulate flowers, which are a tender pink, heavily speckled with brown, and carried in a large well-filled truss. 'Nimrod' flowers with the greatest profusion in April.

Exbury ratings: C, ★ ★ ★

Norman Shaw. g. and cl. AM 1926 (*discolor* × 'B. de Bruin'). A tall, compact, densely clad shrub with rich pink flowers in a good, shapely truss. A good plant for flowering at the end of June and into July.

Exbury ratings: B, ★ ★

Octavia. g. ('Akbar' × *griersonianum*) 1947. A shrub of average size and good habit, bearing red flowers in a well-packed truss. May–June.

Exbury ratings: C, ★

Octopus. g. (*dichroanthum* × *kyawii*) 1950. A shrub of rather low stature, spreading widely, with loose trusses of orange flowers. June.

Exbury ratings: C, ★

Oklahoma. g. ('Bellerophon' × 'Tally Ho'). As the shrub received an award after the first edition, we describe it more fully in p. 113.

Exbury ratings: C, ★

Old Olson ('Ole Olson'). A clone of Lady Bessborough g.

Olympia. g. ('Day Dream' × *elliottii*) 1947. The male parent makes this somewhat tender. The shrub is of normal size and good habit, with deep green leaves and scintillating, red flowers in an ample and shapely truss. June.

Exbury ratings: D, ★

Operetta. g. (*griersonianum* × 'Ambrose') 1947. Crimson. *n.i.c.*

Ophelia. g. (*callimorphum* × *auriculatum*) 1947. Erect of habit but moderate in height, this shrub bears pure white flowers in a truss of good size and formation. April–May.

Exbury ratings: C, ★

Oregonia. g. ('Gladys Rillstone' × *griersonianum*) 1947. Flowers of rich, deep pink bloom late in an excellent truss on a plant of average size and good habit. June.

Exbury ratings: B, ★

Organdie. A clone of Icarus g.
Oriflamme. A clone of Lady Chamberlain g.
Ottawa. A clone of Lady Bessborough g.
Our Kate. g. and cl. AM 1963. (*calophytum* × *macabeanum*). Named after Edmund de Rothschild's eldest daughter, Katherine Juliette, this is a new rhododendron of the highest order, but needing the best conditions for a broad-leaved rhododendron.

Fig. 14
Floral forms: ventricose and openly campanulate ('Our Kate', AM).

Seed from this cross between two giant Asiatic species did not flower until fifteen years after sowing, but it has now grown into a small tree some fifteen feet high, with large, leathery leaves eleven inches long, coated beneath with a loose indumentum, easily removed by touch. The influence of the parent named after Mr McCabe is therefore obvious. The flowers that result from the marriage are of great beauty, being a very pale pink, flushed with a deeper pink on the margins of the lobes and lit up by a sparkling ruby throat (a description that differs from the RHS citation). They are openly campanulate and inflated in form and are arranged in an impressive, lax truss of some twenty florets.

The shrub has a fine, close-knit habit and handsome bearing and will certainly grow a good deal larger still. Altogether a great acquisition for gardens that provide the conditions it needs. Its season is April.

Exbury ratings: C, ★ ★ ★ ★

Oxlip. g. (*williamsianum* × *litiense*) 1947. This is a charming garden plant, flowering with great profusion and presenting a lively and sparkling spectacle typical of spring. The shrub is of moderate size, admirably close and dense in behaviour, and bearing very pretty small bells daintily poised in loose clusters. They are deep rose in the bud, opening to pale pink and finishing completely white. Thus *R. williamsianum* is dominant in the bell and the neat foliage, but *R. litiense* adds to the stature. A charming colour combination and an excellent shrub for smaller gardens. April.

Exbury ratings: B, ★ ★ ★

Parisienne. g. and cl. (*valentinianum* × *burmanicum*) 1947. This interesting cross resulted in a dwarf shrub of a maximum height of four feet, of dense habit and tender disposition. The flowers are a good yellow, faintly scented, borne in small, rather loose trusses. It flowers abundantly and is very showy in April.

Exbury ratings: D, ★

U.S.: H–5, 2/2

The new clone **Goldfinger,** primrose with an orange patch on the upper lobe, received the AM when shown by Sir Giles Loder.

Paulette. g. ('Bellerophon' × *kyawii*) 1950. A slightly tender shrub of good deportment and normal size with deep green leaves and well-filled trusses of bright crimson flowers. June.

Exbury ratings: D, ★

Perdita. A clone of Halcyone g.
Persimmon. A clone of Golden Horn g.
Philomene. A clone of Iviza g.
Phoenix. g. ('Dawn's Delight' × 'Tally Ho') 1950. A loosely-growing shrub of normal height with red, waxy flowers gleaming in a good truss. May.

Exbury ratings: C, ★

Pinafore. A clone of Barbara g.
Pirate. g. ('B. de Bruin' × *meddianum*) 1940. The deep red flowers are carried in an excellent truss on a tall, well-disposed plant. April–May.

Exbury ratings: C, ★

Prelude. g. and cl. 1942, AM 1951. (*wardii* × *fortunei*). This was the last cross that Lionel ever made (LR1210 in the stud-book) and was exhibited nine years after his death. It ranks among his best in his variations on the theme of yellow, but is not yet widely distributed. The shrub is of middle height and good, solid build, clothed with foliage of a leathery, glossy, deep green, following *wardii*. It produces globular, flat-topped bunches of ten wide-open saucers in the manner of *wardii*, pale shrimp-pink or sometimes coral in the bud, opening to a magnolia-white of a remarkably radiant quality, sometimes marked by a tiny crimson flash in the pale primrose throat.

'Prelude' shows every sign of being a hardy rhododendron. Its flowering season is April–May. At Exbury it is very highly rated among the newer varieties.

British ratings: B, ★ ★
Exbury dissent: B, ★ ★ ★
U.S.: H–4, 3/2

Quadrille. g. ('Sulphur Yellow' × *griffithianum*) 1950. Thirteen years elapsed after the mating before this hybrid was introduced. It is a tall plant of good habit, bearing pale cream flowers in a fairly loose truss. April–May.

Exbury ratings: C, ★

Quaker Girl. g. (*hyperythrum* × 'Avalanche') 1950. This mating between a big hybrid and a little species resulted in a shrub of medium height and loose growth, bearing good trusses of large individual flowers, which are white, spotted with green. April–May.

Exbury ratings: C, ★

Quaver. g. (*leucaspis* × *sulfureum*) 1950. This cross almost inevitably led to a dwarf shrub, of spreading and dense habit. The flowers vary from cream to primrose and are borne in small bunches. Very free-flowering and attractive and a good little plant for small gardens with a little shelter. April. See also p. 113.

British ratings: C, ★

Queen of Hearts. g. and cl. AM 1949. (*meddianum* × 'Moser's Maroon'). Nearly the last of L. de R.'s crosses (LR1193). One of the finest post-war rhododendrons, 'Queen of Hearts' is a very striking shrub and an object of deep and moving beauty when in full bloom. Again 'Moser's Maroon' has been introduced to accentuate depth of colour in the red.

The parentage ensures a shrub of convenient size, ten to twelve feet high, fairly close in structure in normal situations. The leaves are dark green, four and a half inches long, with strongly marked veins and a thin, loose, very pale fawn, almost lemon, indumentum beneath. The truss is dome-shaped and is composed of some sixteen open-mouthed bells of a gorgeous, glowing deep crimson, delightfully sprinkled with a number of little black dots and dashes on the upper lobes of the corolla and enlivened with white filaments. The red calyx has large, acuminate lobes. The shrub flowers profusely in the season April–May, when the branches become bent down by the weight of blossom.

In spite of its formal British rating, 'Queen of Hearts' is completely frost-hardy and in the United States has withstood a temperature of 27° below freezing-point Fahrenheit.

British ratings: C, ★ ★ ★
U.S.: H–4, 3/2

Querida. g. and cl. 1950, AM 1952. ('Red Night' × *elliottii*). LR717 in the stud-book. Another first-class red rhodo of recent introduction. The flowers here, in the form of wide open bells, are a brilliant, deep scarlet, darker on the outside, but with a polish that glitters in the sun, marked with a light brown freckling within. Up to sixteen florets are carried in a well-packed truss of rounded form. The plant is tall, growing in a loose and open manner, and has large, deep green leaves, ten inches long. A splendid plant for larger gardens in the right conditions. April–May.

Exbury ratings: C, ★ ★ ★

Quiver. g. (*ciliatum* × *lutescens*) 1950. As one might expect, this is a rather dwarf plant, small-leaved and close-growing. It is somewhat tender, but blooms with the greatest freedom with cream flowers of much beauty composed in small bunches. An attractive plant in April–May.

Exbury ratings: D, ★

Repose. g. and cl. 1950, AM 1956. (*lacteum* × *discolor*). This is an exceptionally fine rhododendron of recent introduction. The plant is medium to tall in stature, with a good habit of growth and foliage that follows *lacteum*. The large bell-flowers, of great distinction, are creamy-white flushed with green and speckled in the throat with spots of greenish-crimson, giving an overall effect of pale lemon. They are carried in a superb, airy, flat-topped truss of some eighteen florets.

'Repose' was introduced by Edmund de Rothschild in 1950 but gained its AM when shown by Slocock's Nursery. May. See 'Welcome Stranger', p. 113.

British ratings: C, ★ ★ ★

Retreat. g. 1936 (*eriogynum* × Lowinsky hybrid). A tall, loose shrub with red flowers shading to pink borne in a good, full truss in May. Of no great merit.

Reverie. g. (*auriculatum* × 'St Keverne') 1950. A big shrub of fairly close growth with large flowers of white with a flushing of pink. June.

Exbury ratings: C, ★

Revlon. cl. AM 1957. (*cinnabarinum* var. *roylei* × 'Lady Chamberlain') (Perseverance g.). This crossing back of 'Lady Chamberlain' with its own dominant female parent has resulted in another superlative addition to the brilliant ranks of *cinnabarinum* hybrids. Here we see again the pendular, slim trumpets or tubes, the glossy finish to the corolla lobes, the splendid carriage and the air of distinction.

'Revlon' grows tall and erect, with shining foliage which is densely scaly beneath. The waxy trumpets are a brilliant carmine and are hung together in clusters of seven, so that the whole splendid plant seems to glitter in the filtered sunlight. It is not yet widely distributed, but is assessed at Exbury at a level to challenge 'Lady Chamberlain' itself. It flowers in May, beginning a little before its male parent finishes.

Exbury ratings: C, ★ ★ ★ ★

Rickshaw. g. and cl. ('Golden Horn' × 'Lady Bessborough'). Introduced in 1950, this attractive and distinctive plant received a Preliminary Commendation in 1958. Its brilliant flowers are an uncommon blend of biscuit suffused with orange, deepening in the throat, a colouring usually associated more with azaleas than with broad-leaved rhodos. A small double calyx is inherited from the *dichroanthum* in 'Golden Horn'. They are elegantly arranged in a truss of medium size, borne on a close-growing shrub of average proportions. June.

British ratings: C, ★ ★

Roberte. A clone of Lady Bessborough g.

Romany Chai. g. and cl. AM 1932. ('Moser's Maroon' × *griersonianum*). A tall, lax, seldom elegant shrub bearing rich, terracotta flowers with brown speckling in large and well-filled trusses. Hardier than its cousin 'Romany Chal', but otherwise yielding place to it in excellence. May–June.

Exbury have recently made this cross again and their first plant is a great improvement, but the clone has not yet been named.

Empire Day is a blood-red clone exhibited by Knap Hill.

British ratings: B, ★ ★
U.S.: H–4, 1/1

Romany Chal. g. and cl. FCC 1937, AM 1932. ('Moser's Maroon' × *eriogynum*). One of Lionel's great pre-war successes and a magnificent spectacle in Exbury woods, where it glows like an enormous torch in June. A group close to some Scotch pines makes a thrilling vision when the sun shines upon it, seeming in imagination to set it on fire as the brilliant scarlet trusses are lit up.

'Romany Chal' is a rhododendron of great vigour, building up eventually to a tall pyramid, clothed with very handsome foliage. The blossoms, gleaming, bell-like, are an ardent cardinal red faintly sprinkled with dark spots, and are borne in well-packed trusses of splendid build, which display themselves in June. In America 'Romany Chal' and 'Romany Chai' are assessed as equally hardy.

British ratings: C, ★ ★ ★
U.S.: H–4, 2/2

Farall is a clone introduced by Mr M. Haworth Booth in 1954.

Rosy Queen. A clone of Asteroid g.

Rouge. g. and cl. AM 1950. (Lowinsky hybrid 1249 × *elliottii*). LR985 in the stud-book. This recent introduction is an arresting plant with a dazzling floral quality and excellent performance, but not hardy. The story of its discovery has already been related in Part II. The flowers are a brilliant, incandescent crimson, dappled with light brown in the throat. They are very large, wide open at the mouth, have a fleshy texture and are impressively displayed in terrific trusses in June. The plant is tall and sturdy but of compact structure and is a stunning spectacle when in full flush.

Exbury ratings: D, ★ ★ ★

Salmon Trout. A clone of Lady Chamberlain g.

Salutation. g. (*griffithianum* × *lacteum*). 1953. Another tender variety of some merit. The tall and well-disposed plant bears large, cream flowers arranged in a well-packed truss of good form. May–June.

Exbury ratings: D, ★ ★

Sandling. A new clone of Halcyone g.

Shangri La. g. and cl. 1965. ('General Sir John du Cane' × *griffithianum*). A fine new hybrid of very vigorous, upright but compact growth, bearing large, white flowers with a greenish flush in the throat, composed in a big, well-filled and balanced truss. A good marriage in which both parents are well represented. May–June.

Exbury ratings: B, ★ ★ ★

Simita. A clone of Fred Wynniatt g.

Sir Frederick Moore. g. and cl. 1935, AM 1937. (*discolor* × 'St Keverne'). One of L. de R.'s successes, which has proved its all-round excellence on a fairly wide distribution over the years. It makes a large plant of good disposition and bears large, open flowers of clear pink, with a little crimson spotting, scented and prettily frilled and gathered in an enormous truss. 'Sir Frederick Moore' flowers in abundance in June and is a thoroughly reliable and quite hardy plant.

L. de R. himself described it as having "a fine, bold truss of pink or rose, with no blue—a first-class cross". He named it after the director of the Glasnevin Botanic Gardens, Dublin, and used it occasionally as a parent. See also p. 113.

British ratings: B, ★ ★ ★
U.S.: H–3, 2/1

There are two clones—

> **Mary Roxburghe** is a rather more spreading plant, with a good, large truss of fine pink flowers, introduced in 1954.
>
> Exbury ratings: B, ★ ★
>
> **Charlotte Rothschild,** AM, a new introduction in 1958. Clean pink with crimson spotting.

Solent Queen. A clone of Angelo g.

Solent Snow. The like.

Solent Swan. The like.

Swan Lake. A clone of Blanc-mange g.

Tasco. g. and cl. (*catacosmum* × *griersonianum*) 1966. A new shrub with the characteristics of an Asiatic cross that should be useful for small gardens. It grows only about five feet high and wide and flowers very freely with lax trusses of about six widely campanulate florets, following the female parent, characterized by large, extended calyces. The colour is a deep, self scarlet throughout, not only in the corolla lobes, but also in the styles and filaments, with black anthers. The leaves show the character of both parents and carry a cinnamon indumentum below. 'Tasco' just misses being top class. April–May.

Exbury ratings: B, ★ ★

Fig. 15
Floral forms:
ventricose campanulate
(*R. macabeanum*, FCC).

Trianon. A clone of Fred Wynniatt g.
Tzigane. g. and cl. ('Karkov' × 'Gipsy King'). Introduced May 1966. A new rhododendron of brilliant scarlet-crimson, five-lobed funnels, faintly speckled on the upper lobes and remarkable for their much enlarged, gamosepalous calyces, which are of the same colour and more than half the length of the corolla tube on the upper sector but undercut below, giving the flower a distinct hose-in-hose effect. They are borne in a well-composed truss to the number of fifteen or more on a shrub of good, rather spreading habit, not likely to exceed eleven feet. The sharply pointed leaves are seven to eight inches long, bearing a faint fawn indumentum. April–May.

Exbury ratings: C, ★ ★ ★

Vienna. A clone of Idealist g.

Yvonne. g. ('Aurora' × *griffithianum*). This is a grex that formed a small colony which was one of those "lost" during the war and found tucked away in a distant corner. It was one of L. de R.'s earliest crosses (LR112) but the seedlings flowered spasmodically over a long stretch of years. There are now three out-standing clones. The plants are tall woodlanders but of compact growth and in 'Yvonne' they bear flat-topped trusses of very large, widely opened funnels, which are white, flushed with pink, with a translucent quality aptly expressed in the names of two of the clones. They bloom in April–May.
The clones are:

> **Yvonne Dawn.** The most recent clone to flower and the finest of all. The flowers are very large indeed, with a fleshy texture, and are flesh pink, fading almost to white with age.
>
> Exbury ratings: C, ★ ★ ★
>
> **Yvonne Opaline,** AM 1931. The buds are deep pink, opening to flowers of deep rose on the reverse and a paler rose internally.
>
> British ratings: C, ★ ★
>
> **Yvonne Pearl,** 1925, pale, pearly pink.
>
> **Yvonne Pride,** AM 1948. The huge funnels measure five inches at the mouth and are pale pink, fading nearly to white.
>
> British ratings: C, ★ ★

Zelia Plumecocq. g. and cl. ('Rosy Morn' × 'Crest'). An entirely new rhododendron named after Madame Plumecocq, the sponsor and organizer of the Valenciennes international flower show. It was shown in the British exhibit at Valenciennes in 1962, when it flowered for the first time, and is a variety of the greatest promise. The *souliei* grandparent (through 'Rosy Morn') is very marked in the large, open, saucer-like flowers of yellow tinted with pink, which are held up in a big, well-built truss; while 'Crest' is evident in the foliage and upright carriage. Not yet registered in 1966. May.

Exbury ratings: B, ★ ★ ★

B. Deciduous Azaleas

The origins and chief characteristics of the Exbury azaleas have been outlined in Part II. Officially, they are classified as "Knap Hill" azaleas, having originated in the strain raised by Anthony Waterer at his Knap Hill nursery in Surrey, of which Lionel de Rothschild acquired a number of seedlings. Their form and poise are often suggestive of butterflies "on tiptoe for a flight" (like Keats's sweet peas). They vary in height from four to seven feet when fully grown in normal soils and in autumn give the gardener a second benison from the wonderful colour of their leaves before they drop to rest.

We have mentioned that the "Exbury Azaleas" can be acquired under that term by simple colour selections. The following is a complete list of the Exbury varieties that have been fixed by name and registered with the RHS. All 104 are good and reliable and it is accordingly unnecessary to describe more than their floral colourings, but it may be of interest that those considered at Exbury to be the best are marked §.

The stars denote the merit ratings judged by the RHS. Three stars constitute the highest rating allotted to azaleas. Ratings of the American Rhododendron Society are in brackets. These are in many instances incomplete for all their qualities of hardiness, flower merit and foliage merit; such lacunae are indicated by a dash.

Amber Rain, AM 1958.	Buttercup, with an orange flash. New.
Annabella. ★ (–, 1/–)	Gold, flushed orange and rose, 1947.
Altair	Cream with yellow patch. A Glenn Dale cv. has the same name.
Aurora ★ (H–3, 2/3)	Salmon-pink with orange flare, 1947.
Balkis	Similar to 'Basilisk' but having a larger splash of orange in the throat.
Ballerina ★★ (–, 4/–)	White.
Balzac, AM 1934. ★★ (–, 1/–) §	Brilliant, fiery combination of red and orange.
Basilisk, AM 1934. ★★★ (H–3, 2/3) §	Rich, deep cream with a golden flare in large trusses.
Bazaar (–, 1/–)	Brick-red.
Beaulieu (–, 3/–)	Deep pink bud opening soft salmon, with deep orange zone. Two 'Beaulieu' registrations were made, but this is the one retained at Exbury.
Berryrose, AM 1934 ★★ (H–3, 2/3)	Rose, with yellow splash, a beautiful arrangement.
Brazil ★★ (H–3, 1/3)	Brilliant tangerine, with frilled margins.
Bride's Bouquet ★★ (–, 3/–)	White, flushed pale pink.
Bright Forecast ★★ (H2, 2/3)	Salmon, deep orange flush, scented.
Bright Straw ★ (–, 4/–)	Deep yellow, with deeper patch.
Brimstone ★★ (–, 2/–)	Pale yellow with orange patch.
Canasta (–, 2/–)	Pale orange in bud, opening to gold, flushed olive, scented.
Caprice ★★ (–, 2/–)	Deep pink. 1951.
Cécile ★★ (H–3, 4/2) §	Deep pink buds open to very large salmon flowers with a yellow flare; of great beauty, 1947.
Clarice ★★★ (–, 1/–) §	Very fine pale salmon with orange patch.
Coronation ★★★ (–, 3/–)	Salmon pink.
Corringe ★★★ (–, 3/–) §	Flame.
Crinoline (H–3, 3/2)	White frilled flowers, flushed pink.
Debutante ★	Light carmine-pink with orange patch.

Desert Pink (–, 3/–)	Pale pink with orange patch.
Edwina Mountbatten	Deep yellow. New.
Eisenhower ★ ★ (H–3, 3/4)§	Fiery red with orange patch.
Exbury Apricot	Large and elegant flowers of vivid apricot with an orange flare.
Exbury Pink	Rose-pink, with a dab of pale orange.
Exbury White ★ (–, 1/3)	Large, white flowers with a dab of orange.
Exbury Yellow ★ ★ (–, 3/3)	Primrose, with an orange flare.
Fancy Free ★ ★ (–, 2/–)	Pink with a yellow flare, 1951.
Favor Major ★ ★ (–, 2/–)	Orange, 1947.
Fawley ★ (–, 1/1)	White, flushed pink, 1947.
Fireball ★ ★ ★ (H–3, 3/3) §	Deep red, 1951.
Firefly ★ ★ (–, 2/–) §	Deep orange.
Frills ★ ★ (–, 1/–) §	Orange red, frilled at the margins, 1951.
Gallipoli (–, 1/–)	Rose-pink buds open to very large flowers of tangerine, flushed rose, 1947.
George Reynolds ★ ★ ★ (H–3, 3/3) §	AM, 1936. Enormous flowers of brilliant, buttery yellow, greenish at the heart. Was L. de R.'s starting-point with Knap Hills, and is still one of the finest.
Gibraltar ★ ★ ★ (–, 4/3)	Buds of dusky orange open to very large fringed flowers of rich orange-red; very spectacular. 1947.
Gilbury	Rose.
Ginger (–, 1/–) §	Orange-carmine buds open to brilliant orange with pink undertones with dark lines on the petals; the upper petal a dusky orange. Sometimes a slow starter.
Glowing Embers ★ ★ (H–3, 2/3)	Red, with orange flare.
Gold Dust ★ ★ (–, 3/–)	Bright yellow, 1951.
Golden Dream (–, 3/–) §	Golden yellow, 1951.
Golden Girl ★ ★ ★ (–, 4/–)	Yellow with a deeper yellow patch, 1951.
Golden Glory ★ ★ ★	Bright yellow.
Golden Horn ★ (–, 2/3)	Gold and orange.
Golden Sunset, AM, 1956 ★ ★ ★ (–, 3/3) §	Tender yellow with an orange "sunset" flare.
Gwynnid Lloyd (–, 1/–) §	White flushed pink with a yellow patch.
Honeysuckle ★ ★ ★ (–, 3/3) §	Flesh pink, orange flare.
Hotspur, AM, 1934 (–, 2/–)	Dazzling flame-red with darker markings on the upper petals.
Hotspur Orange ★ ★ ★	Orange-red.
Hotspur Red (H–1, 3/2)	Brilliant red.
Hotspur Salmon-buff	Pale buds open to salmon-buff with a deep orange patch.

Hotspur White ★ ★	White, with a deep yellow eye.
Hotspur Yellow ★ ★ ★ (–, 2/1)	Yellow buds tipped orange, opening to very large, bright yellow flowers, with a dark line on the centre of each petal and the margin slightly flushed pink.
Hugh Wormald ★ (–, 3/–)	Deep golden yellow, with deeper flare.
Icarus ★ ★	Salmon and orange.
J. Jennings ★ (–, 1/–) §	Intense red, 1947. Highly thought of at Exbury but often a slow starter. Unfortunately some inferior forms are in cultivation.
Katanga §	Beautiful deep old-rose, deepening further in the throat with an orange flare. A new break in colour.
Kathleen	Pale salmon with an orange patch, 1947.
Kipps ★ ★ (–, 1/–)	Tangerine, 1943.
Klondyke ★ ★ (H–3, 3/3) §	A wonderful, glowing gold, rivalling 'George Reynolds', 1947.
Knighthood, AM 1943 (–, 2/–) ★ ★ §	Dusky orange buds, opening to brilliant and elegant flowers of orange, flushed red.
Lady Cynthia Colville	Large deep pink with yellow eye. New.
Langley	Pink with a yellow patch.
Lucky Lady	An Exbury hybrid azalea seedling bought and registered by J. D. Zimmerman, New York.
Madeleine ★ (–, 2/–)	Pale pink with a yellow patch, 1947.
Marina (–, 2/–)	Pale yellow with a deeper patch.
Mary Claire (–, 3/3)	A pretty, fresh pink with a yellow patch.
Middle East ★	Deep orange, 1951.
Nam Khan	Excellent, well-built trusses of deep pink. New.
Nancy Buchanan ★ (–, 2/–)	White with yellow patch, 1947.
Night Light (–, 1/3)	White, 1951.
Old Gold ★ ★ (–, 2/3)	An azalea of delightful form and poise in pale orange, overlaid with rose and an orange flare, 1951.
Orient (–, 1/–)	Brick red, with orange patch, 1951.
Oxydol ★ ★ (–, 3/–) §	Very large white flowers with some yellow spotting, 1947.
Pink Delight ★ ★	Deep pink with a yellow patch, 1951.
Pink Ruffles ★ ★ (–, 3/3)	Pink with an orange patch.
Princess Royal ★ (H–3, 3/3) §	Huge white flowers flushed pink with a yellow flare.
Quaker Maid ★ ★	White, edged rose.

Queen Louise §	Pale pink with yellow eye.
Radiance ★	Red.
Renne (–, 2/–)	Flame, suffused yellow.
Rocket ★ ★ (–, 3/3)	Light orange, suffused red.
Royal Command ★ ★ (H–3, 3/3)	Vermilion.
Royal Lodge ★ ★ (–, 2/–) §	Very deep vermilion, darkening to crimson; a wonderful colour but not very generous, 1947.
Sahara	Yellow.
Sand Dune (–, 2/–)	Pink with an orange patch.
Scarlet O'Hara ★ (–, 2/–)	Red.
Scarlet Pimpernel ★ ★ ★ (–, 2/2) §	Obviously, red, 1947.
Silver Slipper, FCC 1963 ★ ★ ★ §	A beautiful white, flushed pink with an orange patch. Exhibited by Waterer, Sons and Crisp.
Soft Lips ★ ★ §	Flesh pink with a pale yellow patch.
Strawberry Ice, AM 1963 ★ ★ (–, 3/1) §	A beautiful azalea, with coral buds that open to flesh pink, with reticulation of a deeper pink and an orange flush; akin to Cécile, 1947. Exhibited by Waterer, Sons and Crisp.
Sugared Almond ★ ★ ★ (–, 3/–)	Pale pink.
Sun Chariot, AM 1963 ★ ★ ★ (H–3, 2/3)§	Buttercup yellow with an orange flush; exhibited by Waterer, Sons and Crisp.
Sunset Boulevard ★ ★ (–, 3/2)	Pale pink.
Sunset Pink ★ (–, 4/–)	Pink with yellow patch.
Sunte Nectarine	Deep orange with a yellow flash. New.
Surprise (–, 1/–)	Cream, flushed pink.
Swallow	Golden. New.
Tangiers ★ ★ (–, 1/–)	Tangerine.
Tessa (–, 1/–)	Bright orange buds open to flowers of vivid buff with red tips and a deeper yellow patch.
Verulam	Deep cream with a yellow patch.

C. Evergreen Azaleas

The general characteristics of the Exbury Kaempferis and their lineage have been outlined in Part II. It is to be noted that *R. oldhamii* appears with certainty in only one cultivar.

Audrey Wynniatt ('Bassett Wood' × *kaempferi*, LR885 in the stud-book). A gay new variation on a popular theme. The flowers are cerise, individually large and borne with great freedom on a shrubby plant that grows to about four feet, with rather hairy leaves.

Exbury ratings: C, ★ ★

Bengal Fire. (*kaempferi* × *oldhamii*, LR441 in the stud-book). A real dazzler, this. The sturdy bush ultimately grows to about six feet, with a wide spread and rather hairy foliage, and is crowded with vivid flowers that are something between "flame" and brick-red. Just a thought on the tender side.

Exbury ratings: B, ★ ★ ★

Eddy. AM 1944, (*kaempferi* × Indian azalea 'Apollo', LR864 in stud-book). Considered at Exbury to be the best of the large-flowered *kaempferi* hybrids. It grows ultimately to about five feet with deep green leaves and it flowers luxuriantly with a multitude of deep red blossoms. In autumn the foliage turns bright red.

British ratings: C, ★ ★
Exbury ratings: C, ★ ★ ★

Fig. 16
Floral forms: tubular campanulate and heavily speckled in purple (*R. irroratum* 'Polka Dot', AM).

Imbros. The "odd man out" here, this is a cultivar of *R. simsii*, acquired from Exbury and shown by Mr Michael Haworth-Booth. It is embellished with large, widely expanded flowers of the tone known as rose-Bengal that measure three inches at the mouth.

Lady Ivor Churchill. (Parentage uncertain). Another new introduction. The plant grows little more than three feet high with a closely-knit formation and bears pink hose-in-hose flowers in great profusion.

Exbury ratings: B, ★ ★

Leo. ('Malvatica' × *kaempferi*?) Named after L. de R.'s youngest son, this is a very hardy variety, low, leafy, spreading broadly, seldom more than three feet high. The most compact of this group. It flowers with most attractive orange-pink blooms and is valuable for its profusion in June. One of the best azaleas for very small gardens.

Exbury ratings: A, ★ ★ ★

Louise. AM 1939 (*kaempferi* × dark-red Indian azalea, LR444 in stud-book). Large flowers of a clear, bright red are borne abundantly on a plant that grows to above five feet with deep green foliage. Good and compact habit and quite hardy.

Exbury ratings: A, ★ ★ ★

Marie. (same cross as 'Louise'). This bears large, hose-in-hose cerise flowers on a bush that may go to six feet. Not as hardy as 'Louise' but very attractive in light woodland.

Exbury ratings: C, ★ ★

Naomi. ('Malvatica' × *kaempferi*?). A beautiful variety of particular value where an azalea flowering in the period June–July is wanted. The flowers are a tender salmon, borne with great freedom on a bush that may go to six feet.

British ratings: B, ★ ★

Exbury ratings: B, ★ ★ ★

Nigella (same cross as 'Nimrod'). Large hose-in-hose cerise flowers. See further under 'Nimrod'.

Nimrod (*scabrum* 'Kanabo' × 'Louise', LR888 in the stud-book). Showy, orange-pink flowers on a bush of moderate size and good, close habit. 'Nimrod' and 'Nigella' are new varieties from the same cross, which, with the possible exception of 'Tamarisk', was the last one that L. de R. made in evergreen azaleas. They are of similar behaviour and are desirable newcomers.

Exbury ratings: B, ★ ★

Pekoe ('Malvatica' × *kaempferi*, LR861 in the stud-book). Another fairly new azalea, of similar behaviour to the others and equally profuse in flowering, but rather more spreading and very well proportioned. The flowers are a bright pink and very showy.

Exbury ratings: B, ★ ★

Pippa (*kaempferi* × *mucronatum*), LR856 in stud-book. A fairly old variety, this, very well known and popular. It stands out from among the pinks and reds in having large amethyst flowers. Easy, gay, decorative and quite sun-hardy. The shrub has a semi-dwarf, spreading habit, the lower branches bearing close company with the earth and serving excellently as a ground cover.

British ratings: B, ★ ★

Authors' dissent: A, ★ ★

Sir William Lawrence ('Hinodegiri' × *kaempferi*, LR298 in stud-book). AM 1958. One of the best of this range, growing relatively tall but closely and compactly, with dark green, glossy foliage and large, soft pink flowers. Very free and fully sun-hardy.

Exbury ratings: A, ★ ★

Tamarisk (*scabrum* 'Mikado' × *kaempferi*, LR887 in the stud-book). Salmon-pink flowers on a medium-size plant of good, compact behaviour. New. See further under 'Nimrod', which it resembles in general style.

Exbury ratings: B, ★ ★

D. Awards to Rhododendron Species Exhibited by Exbury

augustinii var. *chasmanthum*	AM 1930, FCC 1932.
auritum	AM 1931.
burèavii	AM 1939.
caloxanthum	AM 1934.
campanulatum	AM 1925.
campylogynum var. *myrtilloides*	AM 1925, FCC 1943.
carneum	AM 1927.
chaetomallum	AM 1959.
coryphaeum 'Exbury'	AM 1963.
crinigerum	AM 1935.
diaprepes	AM 1926.
dictyotum 'Kathmandu'	AM 1965.
eclecteum	AM 1949.
edgeworthii as *bullatum* (white form)	FCC 1937.
floribundum 'Swinhoe'	AM 1963.
griersonianum	FCC 1924.
gymnocarpum	AM 1940.
irroratum 'Polka Dot'	AM 1957.
keysii var. *unicolor*	AM 1933.
leucaspis	FCC 1944.
lindleyi	AM 1935.
litiense	AM 1931.
lutescens	FCC 1938.
microleucum	FCC 1939.
mishmiense	AM 1940.
nuttallii var. *stellatum*	AM 1936.
oreodoxa	AM 1937.

oreotrephes as *timeteum*	AM 1932.
oreotrephes as *exquisetum*	AM 1937.
pachypodum	FCC 1936.
× *pallescens*	AM 1933.
pectinatum	AM 1935.
pseudochrysanthum	AM 1956.
quinquefolium	AM 1958.
rigidum as *caeruleum*	AM 1939.
rhabdotum	FCC 1934.
russatum	FCC 1933.
saluenense	AM 1945.
scintillans	FCC 1934.
scopulorum	AM 1936.
siderophyllum	AM 1945.
souliei 'Exbury Pink'	FCC 1936.
sperabile	AM 1925.
stenaulum	AM 1937.
stewartianum	AM 1934.
taronense	FCC 1935.
wardii	AM 1931.
wiltonii	AM 1957.
xanthocodon	AM 1935.

E. Introductions and Awards since 1966

Anton Rupert. g. and cl. ('Sir Frederick Moore' × 'Kilimanjaro'). A strapping plant with pink flowers, deeper in the throat. Raised by Edmund de Rothschild and named after Dr Rupert, Chairman of Rothman International.

R. arboreum 'Rubaiyat'. cl. AM 1968. A seedling from the magnificent tree rhododendron, 'Rubaiyat' is a rare clone of this distinguished but not very hardy species and, indeed, is perhaps the least hardy of them all. The tubular-campanulate flowers, up to twenty-one in number, are blood-red, with protruding black anthers and some dark freckles and are assembled in a round, tight truss. They stand out well among the slender leaves, which have a polished upper surface but are coated below with a very pronounced silvery indumentum. The flowers begin to open in mid-winter and are at risk in a severe season. At Exbury 'Rubaiyat' stands in a sheltered place and has so far not been widely distributed.

Before its award, it was known simply as the 'blood-red arboreum' and often won prizes when shown as such.

British ratings: D, ★ ★ ★ ★
U.S.: H–4, 3/4

Churchill. AM 1971. A clone of the renowned Fortune grex (p. 70). It is as fine a plant as its distinguished twin, but the flowers are deep cream with a small patch of red-purple in the throat. Ratings as for 'Fortune'.

Costa del Sol. cl. AM 1969. This was shown before the RHS Committee as 'Joanita' (see p. 84), but appears to be the reverse cross. The two plants are quite different in flower and in habit of growth, 'Costa del Sol' having the low, rounded habit of *caloxanthum*, only six feet high after all these years, and having flowers of a strong yellow-orange, flushed red in the throat.

Dayan. cl. AM 1967 ('Lady Chamberlain' × *concatenans*). The flowers of this distinguished rhododendron are of a strong orange, with a curious grey overtone that gives it a matt appearance. The trusses of eight or nine florets, widely funnel-shaped, hang in a loosely pendant manner which shows the influence of 'Lady Chamberlain' (p. 88) and the whole bearing of the plant is similar to that parent and, indeed, of the latter's parent, *R. cinnabarinum*. The leaf has a purplish mottling.

Edmund de Rothschild. See page 64. It received a well-deserved AM in 1968 and, being carefully watched, may well earn the FCC in time.

Eisenhower. (Deciduous azalea, p. 105.) Highly Commended after trial at Wisley, for which credit can be claimed by John Waterer, Sons and Crisp, who submitted it. Not to be confused with the purple rhododendron 'General Eisenhower'.

Five Arrows. cl. FCC 1967. This is a seedling from the very distinctive, five-leaved, deciduous azalea, *R. quinquefolium*. The flowers, which begin to open in late April, are pure white, heavily flaked with green in the throat. A very picturesque shrub to maybe eight feet. The species itself had received an AM as far back as 1931 when shown by the Dowager Countess Cawdor. 'Five Arrows' is something of a connoisseur's plant, which needs rich soil in fairly open woodland, preferably shielded from cold winds. The original FCC plant suffered severely from the Great Drought of 1976, but it has been layered *in situ* and is receiving special care to preserve it for perpetuity.

The name is taken from the emblem of the international Rothschild family.

British ratings: B, ★ ★ ★

Galactic. This great splendour, described in page 72, was upgraded to FCC in 1970.

Halton. cl. AM 1967 (*lacteum* × 'Naomi'). This is a sibling of the 'Lionel's Triumph' grex (p. 90) and is a very fine plant, closely resembling that splendid creation, except in the colour of its flowers, which have lost the pink flush, leaving a rich cream tinted with green.

The name comes from Alfred de Rothschild's property which had become a Royal Air Force Station.

Exbury ratings: B, ★ ★ ★

Lionel's Triumph. Elevated to FCC, 1974.

R. morii. A selected form of this big species with white flowers, sometimes flushed pink, with crimson spots, was given the AM in 1977, subject to Exbury's choice of a clonal name.

British ratings: B, ★ ★

Oklahoma. cl. AM 1975 ('Bellerophon' × 'Tally Ho'). Although the mating was made by L. de R., this late-flowering hybrid was introduced by Major A. E. Hardy, one of the leading growers of today, and it had to wait a long time for its award. The big truss may hold anything up to twenty-two florets, which are red and distinguished by black anthers and stigmas. The flowering season is June-July and its parentage, through *eriogynum* and *griersonianum,* certifies that it is not very hardy.

Paris. A clone of 'Naomi' g. Preliminary Commendation. Although its flowers, of a light rose-purple, are not quite up to show-bench standard, as a garden plant it is perhaps the finest in this distinguished company. It stands twenty feet high and nearly as broad with good, dark-green foliage covering the plant right down to the ground.

Peter Barber. An invalid registration made after Mr Barber's supervision had ceased at Exbury. The plant is really 'Jalisco Jubilant'.

Quaver. cl. AM 1968 (*leucaspis* × *sulphureum*). An attractive dwarf with the *leucaspis* habit of growth and well proportioned in all its parts. It has small, elliptical leaves, small trusses of about five small but wide-open bells in an engaging shade of yellow-green, offset by black stamens. 'Quaver' is not very hardy and its flowers, beginning perhaps in March, may get frosted, but others follow.

Red Rock. A clone of 'Gibraltar' g. (p. 73); AM 1970 when exhibited by Major A. E. Hardy. At the present stage of development this is scarcely to be distinguished from the other clone, 'Bastion', but may be of superior quality.

Exbury ratings: C, ★ ★ ★

R. rigidum 'Louvecienne'. AM 1975 but name (after much discussion) not registered until 1978. This selection varies from the wild species in having white flowers with chestnut speckling. It is a dense, twiggy plant, rarely more than seven feet high, thronged with small trusses.

British ratings: C, ★ ★
U.S.: H–4, 3/4

Sir Frederick Moore. (p. 101). Promoted to FCC 1972.

Stanway. AM 1971. A clone of 'Fred Wynniatt' g. (p. 71) and perhaps the best of them all. The rich, deep-yellow flowers are deeper still in the throat than in the lobes and a pronounced bar runs down each petal in the same manner, but not the same colour, as in the other clone 'Joyful'.

The name comes from the birthplace of the late Fred Wynniatt.

Exbury ratings: B, ★ ★ ★

Sun Chariot. This deciduous azalea (p. 107) was awarded the FCC in 1967.

R. vaseyi 'Suva'. cl. AM 1969. In its native North America the deciduous azalea *R. vaseyi* is a pretty pale pink, but in 'Suva' it is red-purple in the bud, paling on opening in early May. A hardy and very welcome addition to the ranks of deciduous azaleas.

British ratings: A, ★ ★ ★ ★

Welcome Stranger. AM 1977. This, one of the most stalwart of the Exbury hybrids, is a clone of the splendid Repose g. (p. 99). It is another example of an L. de R. raising which gained its award when shown by Major A. E. Hardy. The flowers are yellow, deepening in the throat and retaining freckles of 'Repose'.

White Crest. ('Crest × *hyperathrum*). Large bells, pink in the bud, opening white in a loose truss. Registered 1970. Discontinued.

Part Four

Rhododendron Culture

Rhododendron Culture

Given a suitable soil and climate, the culture of rhododendrons in general presents no difficulty whatever. They are a great deal less trouble than roses, rock plants and herbaceous borders and far more trouble-free than apples and pears. They need no annual pruning (apart from the removal of seed pods) and normally they suffer from very few maladies.

Acidity

The soil must be an acid one (with low lime content) unless special provisions are made which are impracticable on a large scale. Opinions differ on which is the ideal pH, but most rhododendrons are content with one of 6 or less. Many have been grown well at 6.5.

There is a common fallacy that the soil must be a peaty one. Peat is excellent for starting root growth, for improving the structure of the soil and for conserving moisture but, except as we shall shortly observe, rotted leaf mould is of at least equal value and, unlike peat, it provides in itself an immediate source of plant food. Gomer Waterer was emphatic that peaty soils were unnecessary and he cited many examples of soil in which rhododendrons flourished, including clay, the stiff loams of part of Cheshire and the alluvial sand and old turf soil of the Manchester area.[1] Some of the best rhododendrons in the country are grown in heavy clay, such as those in the fine garden of Brigadier Otho Nicholson at Privett, in Hampshire, and as at Exbury itself, where there are plenty of clay pockets.

Sandy soils present the problem of water storage, which may in part be overcome by digging in generous quantities of chopped turf (from an acid soil) or by less generous quantities of cow manure accompanied by liberal mulching.

Most inimical of all soils is chalk. Even this can be defeated by building up deep beds of imported lime-free soil, banked up by rock walls, peat blocks or timber baulks, but these mounds and banks dry out very quickly. To make soil pockets in the chalk is of only short-term value, for lime is invasive and will soon infiltrate the new soil.

Climate

The most propitious climates are those in which there is ample rainfall, especially in June and July (when the new buds are forming), and in which the air is to some extent moisture-laden. Like other plants, the rhododendron continuously dispels moisture vapour through the stomata of its leaves and if it diffuses more than it takes in, it will wilt. In the United Kingdom conditions are at their optimum along the greater part of the west coast, in sectors of the south and in Northern Ireland. They are at their lowest level along the east coast and some inland areas.

Nevertheless, many splendid rhododendron gardens are to be found inland,

[1] Rhododendron Association *Notes*, Vol II

Fig. 17
Floral forms: open
saucer-shaped (*R. souliei*,
not FCC form).

but in such places discretion may need to be exercised in the choice of varieties and species. Where other factors are favourable, much can be done, as at Exbury, to remedy nature's deficiencies by artificial watering. In gardens that are not of a scale to warrant their own boreholes, the installation of a ring main, with frequent take-off places for sprinklers, is well worth the expense. If alkathene tubing is used, the expense is not large and the labour of laying it is minimal.

A precept a thousand times repeated is that rhododendrons should never be watered from an alkaline supply. According to report, rhododendrons do appear to have been lost in this way, as is related of that great gardener, the late E. A. Bowles, in his celebrated garden in north London. It is, however, worth recording

118

that, in the three-month drought in England in 1959, the late Francis Hanger, when appealed to by the owner of a small Surrey garden, whispered conspiratorially: "Turn the hose on."

The advice was taken in desperation and with misgivings, but no ill effects followed and this garden has ever since been regularly watered by this means. Yet the supply comes from the pure chalk of the North Downs, is of a high pH (as measured by the Water Board analyst) and, at times, when the sprinklers are taken off the hose, a chalky deposit trickles out. Nonetheless, this is a single experience from which it would be most unsound to draw any general conclusions and the gardener in any similar plight would be very well advised to experiment on a small scale, though in sandy soils it would probably be quite safe. It follows that in very small gardens the maximum provision should be made for storing rainwater.

This need for a liberal water supply does not mean that the rhododendron would enjoy swamp conditions. Only a few, such as *R. hippophaeoides*, will put up with a waterlogged soil. The first requirement, as in nearly all fields of husbandry, is good drainage.

Climate has further to be considered in relation to frost. As we have seen, many rhododendrons will not stand very low temperatures, a frailty which debars many of the most beautiful from the colder localities of the United States, where, however, those that have North American sap, such as *R. catawbiense*, or others such as the old 'Cunningham's White', will stand considerable freezing. The British and American hardiness ratings are a good, though not infallible, guide in this matter. In many instances the plant itself is hardy enough, but not its buds. This applies particularly to those that flower very early in the year. The autumn buds may look fat and full of promise but may be blasted or withered by a hard February frost. The popular and pretty 'Cilpinense' is a familiar example, as also are *R. moupinense*, 'Bric-a-brac' and 'Bo-peep', among others.

Frost tenderness and drought tenderness may both be modified by the leafage of overhanging or adjacent trees. This may slightly mitigate the severity of frost and certainly reduces loss of moisture in the rhododendron by transpiration. It also prevents bleaching of the blossom colour, to which many rhodos are prone in full exposure. Excessive tree cover, however, causes the rhododendron to be much drawn up and straggly, causes root competition in the struggle for water and prevents the hardening of branches by the sun, which, in turn, is necessary to withstand winter cold. "Dappled sunlight" (to repeat a much-used phrase) is thus the condition to aim for in general cultivation (except for those with a hardiness rating of "A") and this is certainly the setting, as at Exbury, in which rhododendrons look pictorially most beautiful.

However, one has only to visit almost any great garden (as Exbury itself), or any large public park, to see rhododendrons entirely happy in the full glare of the sun. As Gomer Waterer noted, wind is more damaging than sun. In open positions one may safely plant all those that are rated "A", such as 'Purple Splendour', 'Jacksonii', 'Fastuosum Flore Pleno', 'Blue Peter', 'Sappho', 'Bagshot Ruby' and many more, all easy and reliable rhododendrons, together with several of the species, such as *discolor*, *orbiculare*, *campanulatum* and many of the dwarfs.

The number of hybrids officially rated as "A" is surprisingly small, but fortunately plenty of those rated as "B", given enough water to drink, are quite happy under the same conditions, though their blossom may not last quite so long or may bleach a trifle. Examples are 'Cynthia', 'Britannia', Lord Swaythling's fine red 'David', 'Scandinavia', 'Doncaster', 'Betty Wormald', 'Susan', 'Goldsworth Yellow', 'Naomi' and all her charming brood, the celebrated 'Pink Pearl' and its likes. To these are to be added most of the azaleas, both deciduous and evergreen, and we may now also add the entirely new 'Nicholas' from Exbury.

Thus, to sum up, we may say that, for rhododendrons in general, the best preliminary conditions are an acid soil, good drainage, ample rain, dappled or oblique shade and a locality in which the thermometer never falls below 10° F, for other than short periods.

The Soil and the Plant

We have discussed the provision of water and the selection of a suitable site, either woodland or open ground. However excellent these conditions may be, they will avail nothing unless the young rhododendron is given the best possible start in life. It may quite possibly outlive the gardener and good sense demands conscientious preparation.

The first requirement, as we have briefly noted, is good drainage. While the soil must be of a nature and structure to retain moisture in its upper levels, excess water must be able to drain away freely. A water table within fifteen inches of the soil is likely to result in many losses. Thus, if the ground does not release excess water naturally, artificial drainage must be provided.

The next requirement is to dig the selected ground all over (not merely selected pockets) two spits deep by the process of double digging, breaking up the bottom spit with the fork and keeping it at its own level. This will assist drainage and aerate the soil. Into the top spit should be incorporated liberal quantities of peat or decayed leaf mould of oak or beech. How much to use will depend on the nature of the soil. On rich, loose, loamy soils all that is needed is sufficient to assist the rhododendron's fine rootlets to make an easy start in the earth; the equivalent, one may say, of two bucketfuls per square yard. In clay soils, in which the physical action of peat is so important, and in sandy soils, in which water drains away too quickly, twice that amount may be needed in the initial digging. In clay soils peat has the effect of liberating acids which precipitate the clay colloids, thus reducing the obstinate sticky quality and, by holding the soil particles apart, gives the roots of the rhododendron an easy run. In light, sandy soils the addition of chopped-up turves, in both spits, ameliorates the disadvantages.

In good, rich loams or in old forest land deeply bedded with decayed leaves, no manure or fertilizer is necessary, or even desirable. A soil too powerfully stimulated may result in rapid growth with abundant foliage, but few flower buds. In clays and sands, however, a moderate dosage of cow manure, not too raw and well mixed in to the top spit, will improve physical conditions and augment food supplies. This seems to be particularly important where peat is used generously, for in itself it has no food value. Horse and pig manures are not recommended.

This initial preparation of the ground ought to be carried out some weeks before the rhododendrons are to be planted. It should then be left undisturbed and no account trodden on. A loose, well-aerated soil should be the aim. If access to the ground is essential, treading boards should be used and the soil pricked over afterwards.

The leading rhododendron nurseries are usually to be relied upon to send out good, well-branched and healthy plants, but the customer who is particular, especially if he wants specimen sizes, is well advised to visit the nursery himself and select his own plants. In the broad-leaved species and varieties, he should look for plants that are well branched at the base, having not fewer than four main branches and being reasonably well set with flower buds. The best time to make this inspection is September, when the plants have finished their growth and should be in shop-window condition.

A visit when the plants are in bloom in April, May or early June may help to resolve one's doubts of the varieties or species to choose, but will give no idea of

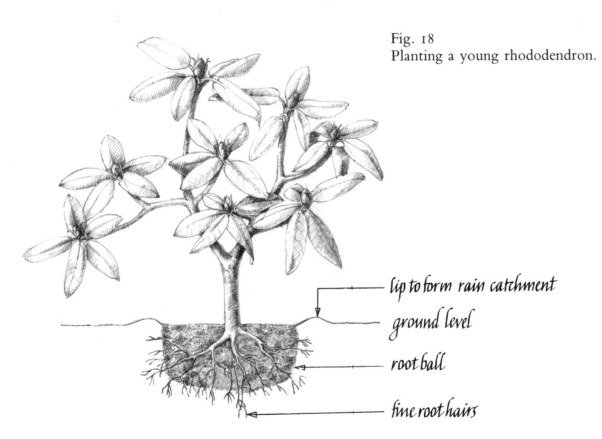

Fig. 18
Planting a young rhododendron.

lip to form rain catchment

ground level

root ball

fine root hairs

the dimensions to which the plants will grow. Mature plants may be seen in the big private and public gardens, but are seldom adequately labelled. For those who have the time, it is important to find a good "form" of a plant, for they may vary considerably. The 'Temple Belle' of one nursery may be very inferior to that of another.

Today it becomes more and more difficult to buy rhododendrons of "specimen" size, so heavy is the demand. The impatient gardener (and the gardener who has passed the half-way mark in life's span usually is) may have to search far and wide for bushes that will quickly fill up those large blanks in his new beds. A visit to a nursery, however, may well yield a well-grown 'Carita' when he had been thinking of a 'Naomi' or a fully-fledged 'Idealist' when he had had in mind a 'Unique' or a 'China'. In the state of things as they are, he will not very often get a plant more than a couple of feet high, if that, but his consolation will be that he has saved some money.

Arrange with the nurseryman an approximate date of delivery, to ensure that the plants do not arrive when there is no one to receive them. Planting can be done at any time between October and mid-April inclusive, provided that the ground is not frost-bound or heavily sodden. Probably the optimum month is October when the soil is still warm.

On arrival, the root-balls of the plants will be found to be tied up either in sacking or in an open-meshed net. The former must be removed at the moment of planting but the net may be left on. Estimate the size of hole needed for each plant. Dig it wider than seems necessary—several inches wider all round for a large plant, three or four inches for a small one—but no deeper than the root-ball itself. Apply peat very liberally all round the circumference of this hole, mix it up with the soil and apply a little organic food to offset the lack of it in the peat. This may be hoof-and-horn meal or a fish manure such as Eclipse (which is very acid) or a seaweed fertilizer. Bonemeal is sometimes advised, but most bonemeals seem to be alkaline and so are perhaps best avoided; opinions differ.

The hole having been appropriately shaped after this treatment, plant the rhododendron in it. If the hole has been neatly judged, the top of the root ball will be level with the soil. If it is below that level, lift it and build up the hole from the bottom. If it is a trifle above the soil level, no matter. All rhododendrons are shallow-rooting and the greatest mistake that can be made is to bury the whole root-ball. In heavy soils, in fact, the root-ball is best only three-quarters buried, and then topped up with a mulch, as we shall shortly see.

A minor but important requirement is to be sure that the tips of the fine roots are in intimate contact with the new soil into which they have to grow, particularly the peat. For this purpose the soil on the nursery root-ball may have to be teased out until the roots are visible for half an inch or so. If this is not done, the roots may be reluctant to venture beyond their ball, with the result that the plant puts on poor growth.

After making the plant comfortable in its new home, it has to be very firmly settled into it. The commandment constantly repeated is that it should be well trodden in underfoot, "with the full weight of the heel." No doubt this is good advice in light, sandy soils, but in heavier ones there is the serious danger that the soil will be compacted, forming a barrier to the passage of water, which is really the young plant's first need. There is also the danger of damaging the roots.

Accordingly, it may be thought a better policy to give the plant only a light firming with the hands followed by a good long drink of rainwater and to defer the final firming for a day or more. In very dry soils two or three waterings may be needed before final firming, which must not be done too soon after watering, or else a squelchy condition of the soil occurs. As building engineers know, water itself is an excellent "punner" of the soil. After it has soaked in well, the final firming need not be so severe as to compact the soil or to damage the roots. The concept of a loose, well-aerated soil must always be in mind.

The amount of spacing between plants will depend, of course, on their ultimate size. For very large sorts, such as 'Polar Bear', 'Loderi', 'Avalanche', the species *macabeanum*, *discolor*, etc., the distances will need to be measured in yards. For those of normal stature and spread, which comprise the majority, six feet is enough. For those of more modest and compact growth of the like of 'Red Cap', 'Cilpinense', 'Burning Bush', 'Bo-peep', 'Blue Bird', 'Fandango', the species *haematodes*, *moupinense*, *neriiflorum*, etc., a spacing of three feet six inches would suit. For *R. williamsianum*, 'Elizabeth', Carmen', and most azaleas a foot less. The alpines and dwarfs are fairly safe at two feet apart or even less. All, if they run into one another, can readily be lifted and transplanted.

After planting and watering, the next care is mulching or top-dressing. This excellent practice, in which we copy and improve upon nature's methods, has four principal virtues: it helps the soil to retain moisture in summer, helps in the suppression of weeds, rots down into natural plant food and provides a comfortable winter blanket. A recommended practice is to mulch with peat immediately after planting to a depth of two inches or so and thereafter, every year or every other year, to lay on a thick mulch of leaves—oak, beech and other thin-textured sorts, not chestnut, sycamore or ash—to a depth of anything up to a foot, except, of course on dwarf sorts.

If the leaves are imported from some garden other than one's own, they had better be from trees grown on lime-free soils, for leaves from limy soils (we are told) bring lime with them. Leaf mulches are best applied in late autumn. Bracken, where available, is also an excellent mulch, applied at the same time, and this is the practice in the RHS Garden at Wisley. In the United States and Canada pine-leaves and the decayed tissues of Douglas fir are much used.

These mulches, however, if thick, tend to de-nitrify the soil until the beneficent soil organisms have done their work on them; these organisms have to rob the soil itself of the nitrogen they themselves need. It may therefore be desirable to spread a nitrogenous fertilizer, in moderate quantities, on the soil surface before applying the mulch. Dried blood is good for this and so are the other organic fertilizers mentioned before. These are longer lasting than sulphate of ammonia (which should not be used on sticky clays, making them more sticky).

In very prim gardens, leaf and bracken mulches are often objected to, as they "look untidy" and get scattered by winds and birds. This is an issue one must resolve for oneself, but a great deal can be done to keep the leaves off paths and lawns by surrounding the beds with belts of wire netting, about eight inches wide, which are obtainable from builders' merchants and are very unobtrusive. Your true gardener is always happy when he sees his plants comfortably tucked up in a russet blanket.

Inevitably this spacing will leave large gaps in the beds for the first few years. How to fill them may not be an easy problem, especially in woodland gardens, unless one is prepared to scrap a great deal of what one plants as the rhododendrons develop. For spring there are always bulbs, which, if not planted too close to the rhododendrons, may remain indefinitely until the time comes to lift and divide them. For summer there are lilies, which associate very happily with rhododendrons and even more so with the dwarf evergreens and semi-evergreen azaleas, which help to keep their roots cool. The dwarf azaleas also marry most successfully, and for life, with floribunda roses, especially those of the less strident hues. *Galtonia candicans*, like a monster white hyacinth, is suitable among any kind of rhododendron and so are hostas in their many fine leaf forms.

The lively berries of *Pernettya mucronata*, which sparkle so brilliantly in autumn and which spread into thickets where they are happy, are natural associates; so also, in open, sunny beds, are all manner of heathers, which are cousins of the rhododendron. Gaultherias and skimmias will not fill the spaces quickly enough, unless planted densely and uneconomically, but the beautiful prostrate roses will do so most decoratively by the second year and, to boot, they will very effectively suppress weeds. These "scramblers" include the *rugosa* hybrid 'Max Graf', the *macrantha* hybrid 'Raubritter', *Rosa* × *paulii* 'Rosea' and *R. wichuraiana*.

Less expensively, one can plant helianthemums and halimiums if the situation is sunny. Primroses, forget-me-nots, *Tiarella wherryi*, *Cornus canadensis*, lady's mantle (*Alchemilla mollis*), rosemary and so on are other inexpensive consorts that will soon fill the blanks and some of them can well stay there when the rhododendrons are full-grown.

Maintenance

For the rest of their lives, the overriding need of the rhododendron is water, on which enough has already been said.

An annual chore is to remove the seed pods as soon as possible after the flowers are over. The process is simple, though tedious where there are a great many plants. Using thumb and finger, the whole truss—not merely the individual foot-stalks—is snapped off by a sideways and downwards pluck. The only peril is damage to the young growth-buds which are likely to be showing immediately below the truss and in the axils of the topmost leaves. However, on broad-leaved rhodos, it is easy enough to snap the stem off immediately above this point.

Few people have the patience to perform this dead-heading operation on the dense, dwarf evergreen azaleas and their kind, or on other small rhodos that flower in similar close profusion, such as the species *russatum*, *radicans*, *impeditum*, *scintillans* and so on, or even 'Blue Tit' and 'Carmen'. Indeed, more harm than good can be done unless great care is taken.

An important point in cultivation is to avoid damage to the fine roots that lie close to the surface. This means forbidding use of the spade, fork and trowel and using even the hoe with great circumspection, merely skimming the surface when weeding has to be done.

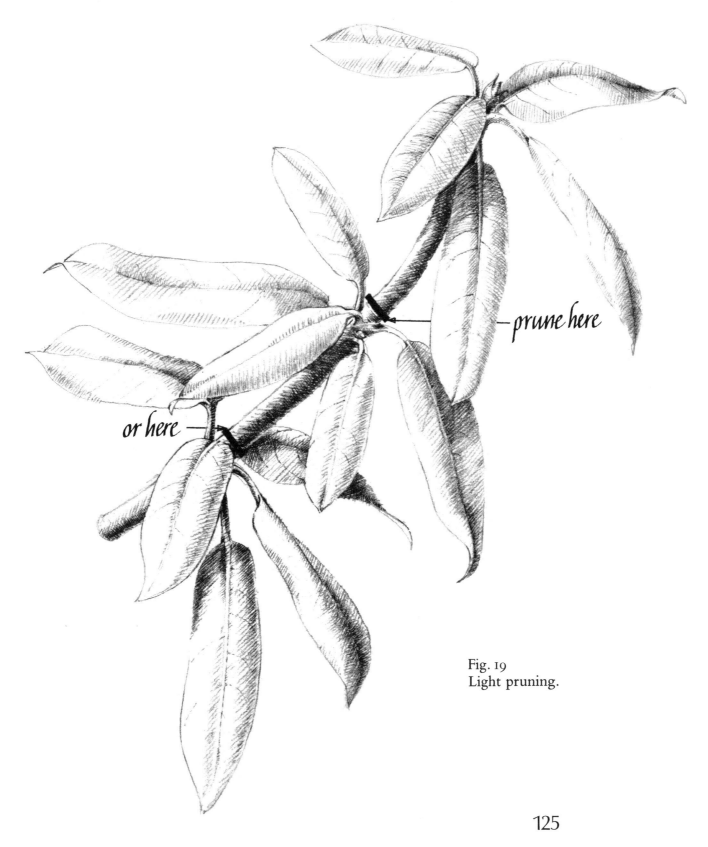

prune here

or here

Fig. 19
Light pruning.

125

On plants that have been grafted, keep a lookout for the growth of suckers from below ground level. These should be roughly removed, not with knife or secateurs, but with a sharp snatch at the point of origin on the understock or its roots. Neglected suckers that have become tough can be chopped off, at the same point, by a blow with the draw hoe or spade.

Rhododendrons can freely be transplanted at almost any size, the only practical restriction being that of physical effort. With knowledge and care, they can be lifted in full flower, and often are for the Chelsea Flower Show; but normally the right seasons and circumstances are the same as those outlined for their initial planting.

For a plant of modest size, say up to three feet six inches, it is sufficient to cut all round with a sharp spade, then undercut and lever the plant out with a good ball of soil. The roots must be cleanly cut, not torn, so that a spade must be used, not a fork, and the cut must be continuous; the fork may, however, be useful for levering and lifting out, especially if the job is too much for one man.

The distance from the stem at which the circular cut is made depends upon the size of the plant. On the specimen mentioned a radius of about fifteen inches from the stem would be appropriate and a second pair of hands would probably be necessary. The plant should be lifted on to a sack to carry it to its new position.

Small specimens are very easily dealt with. Larger ones need to have a narrow trench dug out all round so that the undercuts may be made, the plant being heeled over first to one side and then to the other and the sack insinuated beneath.

Pruning

Rhododendrons seldom need pruning, but are readily amenable to it when necessary. The need may arise:

when a plant has grown gaunt and leggy, lopsided or otherwise mis-shapen;

when its growth is thin and spindly instead of compact;

when a branch has been damaged;

when (particularly in smaller gardens) a very vigorous variety needs to be kept within bounds.

The time for any such pruning is from early April to mid-June according to climate, the earlier the better.

If only a light pruning is required, the task consists merely in cutting back to a point about a quarter of an inch above one of the whorls or rosettes of leaves growing from each stem, as shown in Figure 19.

Where it is necessary to cut further back a leggy plant that has discarded its lower leaves, it is sufficient to amputate at random, watch for the emergence of new leaves and trim any superfluous snags back to that point. Such pruning can be quite drastic, even to the point of cutting back to within two feet of the main stem.

A more expert method is to examine the bark with a magnifying glass to find the faint ring left by an old leaf scar accompanied by the minute swellings in the bark made by dormant buds beneath it. The pruning cut is made immediately above this point.

A few rhododendrons do not respond to the spur of the pruning knife. Examples are: 'Bagshot Ruby', 'Alice', 'C. B. Van Nes', 'Mrs C. B. Van Nes', *R. thomsonii* and its hybrids, *R. lacteum* and *R. calophytum*.

Lopsided growth may sometimes be due to the emergence, at the end of a stem, of only a single new growth bud, which may develop into an unduly long

Fig. 20
Dead heading. Snap off this complete truss of seed pods at the thick black line without harming the young growth buds immediately below it.

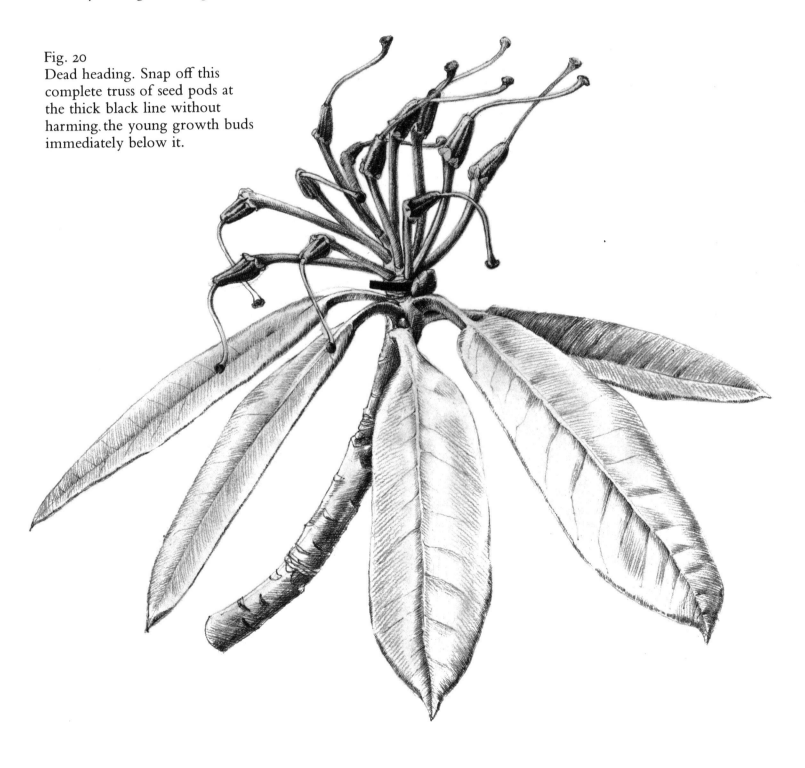

127

extension. After a plant has flowered and its truss of seed pods removed, notice should be taken of the new growth buds that appear below the truss. If there is only one such bud, it should be plucked off. The result to be expected is the emergence of two or more buds that have been lying dormant in the leaf axil.

Ailments of the Rhododendron

As we have observed, the rhododendron has few enemies in nature. Its maladies are chiefly physiological, caused by attempting to rear it in unsuitable conditions: bad drainage, too little water, too much frost, too deep planting, too much direct sun or an unsuitable soil.

Chlorosis

Deficiencies or excesses in the soil soon show themselves in discolorations of the leaf. Should these appear, it is best to get technical advice rather than attempt one's own diagnosis and doctoring, but the condition usually known as "lime-induced chlorosis" is fairly easily recognised and usually not difficult to rectify on a small scale. The symptom is that the leaf turns some shade of yellow, except for the veins, which remain green. The ailment is analogous to anaemia in man and animals.

One constantly says that rhododendrons dislike limy soil, but it would perhaps be more exact to say that they dislike one from which they cannot extract soluble iron, and what lime does is not, as often said, to "poison" the plant, but to act as a chemical barrier to the absorption of iron. Iron acts as a catalyst in the production of the green chlorophyll of the leaves, which is vital to growth. Rhododendrons showing this form of chlorosis are therefore suffering from iron starvation, but we must remember that a certain amount of calcium is necessary for rhododendrons.

The usual reason is simply that the soil is too alkaline, but even an acid soil may have an iron deficiency. On a small scale the ailment can be cured by dressing the soil with an iron sequestrene. Some years ago W. J. Bean remarked on the success of rhododendrons on soils with a strong impregnation of iron, citing those of Mr Kenneth McDouall at Logan and of Sir George Holford at Westonbirt.

Other soil elements of which a deficiency may affect the health of the rhododendron and display themselves by discolorations of the leaf are nitrogen, potassium, phosphorus, magnesium and the "trace elements" required in small quantities, of which iron and manganese are two. In all such matters technical advice is most desirable.

Bud Blast (*Pycnostysanus azaleae*)

This distressing malady is widespread in some regions. Beginning in early autumn, and very prominent indeed by springtime, the young, green flower buds shrivel and turn dark brown, slightly bristly to the touch and looking rather like small larch or pine cones.

It is now established that the disease is a fungus spread by the leaf-hopper

(*Graphocephala coccinea*), though not all seem to be infective. The female insect makes incisions in the buds in July-August and lays her eggs within. Pluck off and burn all diseased buds; do not drop them on the ground.

To prevent recurrence, spray the whole shrub with a systemic insecticide about the 1st July and again a fortnight later. Alternatively, spray with BHC fortnightly until September.

White Fly (*Dialeurodes chittendeni*)

The rhododendron white fly is a small, frail, pallid creature. It is not a serious menace, but the larvae, infesting the under surface of the leaves, secrete a honey-dew which drops on to the lower leaves, resulting in a "sooty mould" which impairs the leaf functions and saps the plant's vitality. The creatures seem to avoid the sorts that have a hairy surface below. They lay their eggs at midsummer, but their slight depredations are not noticeable until the next spring. The similar creature, *Pealius azaleae* attacks azaleas. In both cases spray at midsummer with a systemic insecticide or with gamma-BHC on the lower surface of the leaf.

Weevils

Several species of weevil prey on rhododendrons, the adults nibbling the leaves and their larvae the roots. They spend the day hidden under leaves and débris on the ground and make their attack at night. In America, where weevils and beetles appear to be more damaging than in Britain, a poison bait is widely used. Collect and burn all rubbish and drench the soil with fenitrothion or other soil insecticide.

Rhododendron Bug (*Stephanitis rhododendri*)

Another tiny, frail creature that sucks the "soft underbelly" of the leaf, from May onwards. It reveals itself by a speckling of the upper surface of the leaf, caused by its sucking apparatus, and a chocolate spotting underneath. Spray with a systemic insecticide in mid-May.

Leaf-spot

Purple spots, becoming brown. If widespread, spray with captan or zineb three times fortnightly. Feed the plant well.

Petal-blight

A fungus causes the flower to collapse in a slimy mess. Pick off and burn and spray with benomyl (e.g. 'Benlate').

Azalea gall

A fungus causing fleshy swellings, pink or greenish-yellow turning white. Burn affected members. If widespread, spray with zineb.

Rust

Orange pustules, later brown, on the reverse of the leaf. If widespread, spray with zineb or ferbam.

Principal Sources

Rhododendron stud-books of Lionel and Edmund de Rothschild.
Dr H. R. Fletcher: *The International Rhododendron Register*.
Royal Horticultural Society: *The Rhododendron Handbook*, Vols. I and II.
Rhododendron Association: Year Books.
Rhododendron Society's *Notes*, Vols. II and III.
American Rhododendron Society: *Rhododendrons For Your Garden*.
American Rhododendron Society: Quarterly Bulletins.
Royal Horticultural Society: *Journal*, various articles.
Royal Horticultural Society: Rhododendron and Camellia Year Books.

———

Bowers, C. G.; *Rhododendrons and Azaleas*. 2nd Edition, New York, 1960.
Cox, E. H. M.: *Rhododendrons for Amateurs*. London, 1924.
Cox, E. H. M. and P. A.: *Modern Rhododendrons*. London, 1956.
Leach, David G.: *Rhododendrons of the World*. London, 1962.
Millais, J. G.: *Rhododendrons*. London, 1917.
Street, Frederick: *Hardy Rhododendrons*. London, 1954.
Street, Frederick: *Rhododendrons*. London, 1965.

Index

(Exclusive of the Exbury Register)

DATE DUE			